BEFORE DEATH COMES

Maurice S. Rawlings, M.D.

THOMAS NELSON PUBLISHERS
NASHVILLE

All through history man has been the only creature made aware that he must die. Yet he refuses to believe it until the last moment, when he is usually unprepared.

CONTENTS

PROLOGUE

As night follows day, the time unfalteringly approaches when I must pay for yesterday. Yesterday I was young, not caring what life was all about.

Suddenly bewildered that much of life is rapidly passing, I find my remaining days are very dear to me, with none to waste. No more of them must trickle through my fingers while I discover what truth is all about. Knowing of the experiences of people who have been beyond death's door, I realize I must someday find my own passageway.

I know this passageway is not a materialistic one. I will have to leave my possessions behind; yet my spirit still desires confirmation. Which is the right way through death's door? If I am allowed only one choice, that choice must of necessity be right!

I'll search again today for what I neglected to find yesterday—when I was young. I'll rummage through yesterday in a quest to find tomorrow . . . and you can come with me if you like.

ACKNOWLEDGMENTS

Many people took part in the composition of this book; I have traveled through many lands and through more literature than I care to recall. Some of the people who have contributed to this writing participated as unknowing actors in some scenario; others were interviewed for their opinions. Although I can't thank them individually, they might recognize themselves in the substance of the manuscript.

When I was encompassed by problems beyond my capacity and reason, I called for help from such people as Rev. Matthew McGowan of Central Presbyterian Church in Chattanooga, Rev. Ben Haden of First Presbyterian Church, Nell Mohney, religious columnist for the *Chattanooga News-Free Press*, Kay Arthur and her staff at Reach Out Inc., and Spencer McCallie, Jr., of McCallie School in Chattanooga. Critical comments by Peter Gillquist of Thomas Nelson Publishers and by Dr. Bert Bach, Dean of Faculty at the University of Tennessee at Chattanooga, helped complete this manuscript.

Volumes of research material were untiringly typed and condensed by my devoted secretary, Mrs. Ella McMinn, with supplemental assistance from Mrs. Linda Howard. The patience and forbearance of my seven other physician-partners at the Diagnostic Center and Hospital are certainly appreciated. Since I am a physician and not a Bible scholar, the

ACKNOWLEDGMENTS

aid of my wife and children was solicited in researching the literature of many faiths.

I pray that the reading of this book will challenge you to find your destiny. I know writing it has helped me know mine.

Maurice S. Rawlings, M.D.

Diagnostic Center
Chattanooga, Tennessee
January, 1980

CHAPTER I

Death's Door Revisited

"What's the matter, Honey? Don't you like me?"

"No, and if you don't leave me alone and quit bothering me, I'll yell for my boyfriend!"

"You're alone! I don't see any boyfriend!"

At the far end of the restaurant, walking toward them, was a twenty-one-year-old male who had exited from the men's room. He and his date had come for a snack after the movie. As he returned to the table, he saw the trouble.

Coming to stand between his girl friend and the intruder, the young man tried to look brave even when he saw the knife coming up toward him. The knife was brought gently to the left chest area, as the intruder toyed with an idea. After a moment's hesitation, the assailant made a decision. Leaning a bit on the knife, he watched it glide down through the clothes. He continued, meticulously observing the blade as it gradually scooted for several inches laterally; the blood spurted freely in the wake of the incision. Then he casually withdrew the knife and wiped it clean on the tablecloth as he was leaving.

It was about fifty minutes later when I saw the victim in the emergency room. The ambulance crew had brought him in speedily. His girl friend, who had accompanied him, was trying to hold back tears. The young man was able to talk.

Removing the patient's clothes, we observed a single stab wound between two of his left ribs starting about three inches from the midline, or sternum, and extending for another three inches laterally. There were no wounds elsewhere in the chest or abdomen. His pulse was 130, rapid and barely palpable. His temperature was normal. The respirations were shallow. Blood pressure was 80 systolic. His heart did not seem clinically enlarged, but the sounds seemed distant, difficult to hear. The neck veins were prominently distended, and his general color was palish-blue.

I told the nurse to get the girl friend out of the room. I couldn't hear clearly over her sobbing and crying.

While we were getting the patient ready to be transported upstairs, his respirations became more shallow. He was mentally confused. His neck vein distention had increased, and his blood pressure could only be heard by Doppler technique at 50 systolic.

I quickly inserted a large-bore needle just beneath the lower end of the breastbone and directed it upward toward the left shoulder. I encountered the outer covering of the heart and a lot of liquid blood that didn't belong there—blood that wouldn't clot. Apparently the stab wound had entered into the heart, allowing leakage into the sac covering the heart, called the *pericardium*. There, it compressed the heart as distention occurred, preventing adequate filling; this occurrence is called *cardiac tamponade*, a sure death unless immediately corrected.

After removing a half pint of blood, the patient finally started breathing better, and we thought he was going to make it. But all of a sudden his monitor registered ventricular fibrillation. He convulsed, his eyes turned up in his head, he sputtered and stopped breathing.

"Get the defibrillator charged up," I yelled to the emergency room physician helping me. "I'll defibrillate him while you are getting the endotracheal tube in him."

During the external heart massage the blood kept getting pushed out through the wound, but at least it wasn't accumulating in the pericardium any more. The neck veins were no longer distended.

"Give me the paddles!" I said, referring to the defibrillator.

"Come on, baby—come on back!"

Pressing the red buttons on each handle of the paddles, one over the upper sternum and the other just below the stab wound, I observed the patient respond as his body jumped a fraction of an inch off the examining table.

"We have a pattern," the nurse said. "It looks like sinus rhythm."

"I've got the endotracheal tube in place now," said the emergency room physician. He had been working feverishly trying to find the opening through the vocal cords while the chest and body were being jostled about by the external heart massage.

We did it! He was living. Quickly, we rolled him up on the stretcher to the operating room where the thoracic surgeons, previously alerted, were waiting to close the stab wound in the wall of the heart, stopping further bleeding.

Laboratory personnel arrived shortly with two pints of blood. We stopped the patient's transportation long enough to start a blood transfusion through a needle puncture into a large vein beneath the collar bone. During this procedure, the patient started protesting bitterly of pain—which had not been a complaint previously.

"Why did you bring me back?" he whispered to me. "It was so peaceful! And no pain! I didn't feel any pain at all."

"Just be quiet until we finish getting this blood transfusion started; then we are going to take you up to surgery and get this knife wound repaired," I said.

"But it was so beautiful. I saw my mother and my father!"

A moment passed, and then he volunteered, "I felt myself floating through space. I was going real fast. Then I came to this beautiful city with tall gates, and I had to walk up some stairs to get to them. I could see my parents, but the gatekeeper wouldn't let me in!

"Everything was so beautiful; I have trouble describing it. My parents kept beckoning to me, but for some reason the gatekeeper wouldn't let me through.

"It was at that point I felt you had hit me in the chest with those paddles! And I found myself back in this room, looking up into your face. Why didn't you leave me alone! I am sure they would have let me in!"

Trying to keep him occupied, I told him I was sure they would let him through the gates next time. Then I proceeded to help the crew wheel him to the operating room, where I watched the surgeons proceed to expose the heart. The internal wound was actually quite small, perhaps a one-half inch puncture within the heart wall.

They were able to suture the wound quite easily, staunching the flow of blood.

This patient has talked to me many times since then about his experience. He has not forgotten it, and neither have I.

AFTERLIFE EXPERIENCES

Whether by instinct or desire, I had always wondered about the existence of life after death. *Wouldn't it be marvelous,* I had thought on many occasions, *if we could interrogate someone who actually returned from death? Someone who could possibly tell us what it feels like to die?* Well, it has finally happened! There are now people available who can tell us, people who have been there.

At first I didn't believe it, and it wasn't until I began encountering these afterlife experiences frequently that I began to take them seriously. *They must all be dreams,* I had thought at first. But then I began hearing after-death reports by other doctors whom I met in my travels throughout the country as I was instructing various medical schools in resuscitation courses and establishing advanced life support curricula for the American Heart Association. I would be confronted by doctors and emergency room physicians who had encountered patients who had had experiences similar to the ones I had reported. I thought to myself, *For one, two, or even three people to recount similar dreams would certainly be unusual. But for a large number of resuscitated patients to have essentially the same sequential dream would be impossible.* I concluded the experiences must be real, not dreams.

BEFORE DEATH COMES

People throughout the ages must have wished for the opportunity to talk with someone who could confirm or deny the presence of another life beyond death, the very tenet of most religions. But it has only been in your lifetime and mine—during this present generation—that we have had this very opportunity. Only now has resuscitation been that good! Only now are we afforded the unique opportunity of interviewing a new and growing population of people who have survived clinical death to tell us of a life beyond the grave!

Whereas years ago methods for reviving life after unexpected death were rarely successful, present-day methods are so effective that they will restore life in over half of all sudden deaths. The method is called *resuscitation*. Resuscitation consists of simple methods of breathing and effecting a heartbeat for the patient. The heart contents are pumped intermittently by pushing downward upon the breastbone. No equipment is required except your hands.

Clinical or "reversible" death occurs whenever the heart stops and breathing ceases; the body tissues continue to survive for a few minutes. But without a heartbeat, the body only has four or five minutes survival time before the tissues quickly die, *rigor mortis* sets in, and irreversible death occurs. Clinical death may be turned back by resuscitation, something man is permitted to do without any equipment necessary. *Biological* death—on the other hand—requires a resurrection, something only God can do. So we've never resurrected anyone! We only treat reversible deaths.

Only about twenty percent of persons resuscitated will volunteer an experience in a life beyond; most previously published material recording these experiences has emphasized the "good cases."[1] I have often wondered how many of the remaining eighty percent have had experiences they do not choose to recall. Only those who had attempted suicide reported "bad" experiences to the earlier investigators.

The occurrence of uniformly "good" experiences in the next life sounded, even to me at the time that I first read of these cases, entirely too good to be true. As I reported in Beyond Death's Door,[2] the turning point in my own concepts occurred when a patient experienced cardiac arrest and dropped dead right in my office. Of course, that alone didn't change my thinking, but the fact that this forty-eight-year-old postman was screaming "I'm in hell! Keep me out of hell!" each time he responded to resuscitation efforts did cause me some concern.

Even after hearing this plea, though, my first response was to dismiss it, attributing it to the physical and emotional stress the patient was under at that time. I even told him, "Keep your hell to yourself—I'm busy trying to save your life!" However, as I was attempting to insert a pacemaker into the man's heart through the large vein below the collarbone (to overcome the heart block that would take his life if the pacemaker were not used), he experienced clinical death several times. Each time he regained heartbeat and respiration, he screamed, "I'm in hell!" He was terrified. His fear of this "hell" was greater than his dislike of pain, because

[1]See Elisabeth Kubler Ross, On Death and Dying (New York: Macmillan, 1969); Dr. Raymond Moody, Life After Life (Covington, Ga.: Mockingbird Books, 1975); Drs. Karlis Osis and Erlendur Haraldsson, At the Hour of Death (New York: Avon Books, 1977).
[2]Beyond Death's Door (Nashville: Thomas Nelson, 1978), pp. 17–21.

19

even though my method of external heart massage sometimes fractures ribs, he was telling me, "Don't let go!" He said, "Don't you understand? I am in hell. Each time you quit, I go back to hell. Don't let me go back to hell!"

It finally occurred to me that I had been discarding complaints of dying patients all these years! This man was serious! His face expressed sheer horror. It wasn't just another routine death.

I began to work quickly, but he kept losing consciousness and vital functions. After several death episodes, he finally asked me how to stay out of hell. I didn't really know what to say, but I told him I thought he could say his prayers.

Then he had the nerve to ask me to pray for him! I was insulted! "I'm a doctor, not a minister," I told him. But since he was a dying man, I thought I would humor him. So I prayed for him. He repeated my words. It was a simple prayer: We asked Jesus to keep him out of hell; and if he lived, he would stay "on the hook" for Christ. There was only one problem: The conversion experience "backfired." It not only got him—it got me, too!

Once the pacemaker was in place and the man was taken to the hospital, his condition stabilized. I went home and started reading the Bible to find out what it said about hell. My former belief that death was merely oblivion was being shattered. I was now convinced that there is life after death after all, and that not all of it is good.

Later I went back to the patient who had claimed to be in hell. When I asked him what hell looked like, he said, "What hell? I don't recall any hell." I explained what had happened while he was being resuscitated in my office, but he could not recall any of the unpleasant events. He did remember the prayer, but apparently his hell experiences were so frightening his conscious mind had suppressed them into the subliminal parts of the memory. Instead, he remembered only the "good" experiences that occurred after his covenant with God.

The authors of the earlier books on life-after-death experiences are all psychologists or psychiatrists who have not personally resuscitated *any* of the people they have discussed in their books. They interview other doctors' patients, sometimes days, weeks, or even years following the clinical death episode. They interrogate volunteers. Volunteers report good experiences, not "bad" ones.

Who, for instance, is going to boast about being in hell once they've fully regathered their senses and reasoning? All of us love to tell our friends all about our great accomplishments and successes. Even as children we tried to avoid telling our parents about the "F's" we got on our report cards. We certainly didn't brag about them. But whenever we made "A's," we always brought these to our parents' attention. So it is in adult life. Self-esteem is essential for our mental health. No one cares to admit his failures in this life; and certainly no one wants to admit his being in hell in the life beyond.

As in the so-called good experiences, the bad ones also have a sequence of events: out of the body, through some tunnel or tubular conveyance, and into another world. Here the events are never pleasant. The circumstances are so foreboding that after the persons are resuscitated, they change their lifestyles immediately. In those cases when the revived persons can be closely questioned, these dramatic changes seemed to involve some sort of a religious conversion experience and some sort of a personal commitment of their lives. Their present predicament is too painful to leave unchanged but too embarrassing to confide in others. They are sure their experience was not a dream.

Because these devastating and disrupting "hell" experiences are usually hidden by the ones who have had them from their friends and families, they are best detected at the time of resuscitation or shortly thereafter. Sometimes detection of a pall of severe depression or inappropriate apathy may give a clue that a patient has endured a recent "hell" experience. Depression often may last several days or weeks, as in the following case.

The alarms went off, and I felt myself fainting. I knew my heart had stopped. I just knew it had. I felt it! I saw the nurse run into the room where I was located and fool around with the gadgetry to which I was attached to see if it was working properly. Then she thought that I was dead because she yelled "code 99," and then the other nurse came in. The first nurse started breathing into my mouth and then used this black mask over my face, a big black thing that looked like a football with a mask on it. It made my chest rise, and I would breathe.

I had to walk around past this first nurse to see the other nurse who was pushing on my chest. It made the whole bed shake, and she kept mumbling some numbers to herself, maybe to make the rhythm go right. During all this time, my chest pain had gone, and I was really feeling good.

Then I smiled to myself because I began to realize

that I had someway floated up to the ceiling of the room and I was looking down on them from up there, sort of floating around. But I never felt better! It seemed strange, seeing me on that bed, but I could see it was my face. Gee, I felt funny! I knew I was dead, but I didn't seem to care!

Then things suddenly started getting dark, and I found myself spiralling through space into another sort of world; I was traveling very fast. It was some sort of tube that ended in a black nothing. I felt like I was being sucked into a big, black void. I was getting hotter and hotter as I was approaching a light coming from a side-entrance or a side-hole which led to another tunnel which contained long rows of benches with people sitting on them.

They made me sit at the end of one long bench which seemed to stretch for a long distance and angle into another opening or tunnel which was illuminated by a light brighter than this one. I couldn't see where the light was coming from or what was in the tunnel; so I asked a fellow next to me, but he didn't seem to know either. He was also waiting his turn. Then I noticed a grimy looking guard standing near the entrance, his arms crossed. As another batch of people left the bench in our room to go into the next room, the figure ordered all of us to "move up." Two of the people I saw on the bench I had known in high school. I'm sure of it.

As we moved down the bench, I was close enough to see around into the next passageway, and there in the walls were large doors with iron gratings containing huge fires behind them. Overseers that seemed to have absolute command were rapidly pushing people into these ovens or fires. As one group of people entered, others were moved up by drivers in the rear passageways.

I prayed and prayed, "God help me! God save me!" In some way my name was called out from far above the passageways, vibrating all the way down to where I was sitting. I heard the voice say, "I have called you back. I have need of you!"

The next thing I knew I was back in my body and looking up into the face of the doctor who was making an awful thrust into my chest that made me feel like my ribs were broken. I really didn't care if he broke all of my ribs! I was just glad to be back. I never want to go back to that place! It opened my eyes about how I was living my own life. I've since made a great change. It has made a believer out of me!

For the first two weeks following this event, this patient was withdrawn and didn't try to communicate with his family, his friends, his doctors—or anyone for that matter. He seemed tense, frightened, and not at all eager to relate the story to me the next day after it happened. When I accidentally noticed he had a Bible under the bedcovers, he admitted that he had started reading it. Then he asked me to sit and talk. I learned that he was no longer afraid of the death experience itself. However, he was convinced there was life after death, and he wanted to be sure he would never go back to the "hot-box." Live or die, he said he was going to bet his future life on Jesus Christ. He said he wanted to know he couldn't lose.

I could see his point: If he was wrong, he had lost nothing; if he was right, he had gained everything! Better odds than the stock market! A 100 percent bet!

Unfortunately, he never left the hospital alive. At first he seemed to get much better and was looking forward to returning to his used-car business and starting a new life. But two and a half weeks after the initial cardiac arrest, he had a sudden extension of his heart attack and died. This time resuscitation attempts were unsuccessful. Clinical death soon progressed into biological death—the irreversible death St. Paul must have been talking about when he wrote in the first century, "And . . . it is appointed for men to die once, but after this the judgment."[3]

BEFORE DEATH COMES

All through history man has been the only creature made aware that he must die. Yet he refuses to believe it until the last moment, when he is usually unprepared. This book will make you acquainted with death itself and help you prepare for it.

First of all we will examine the dying process itself. You will learn what it feels like to die. We will look at the institutions we have created—hospitals, nursing homes, hospices—to take care of those who are "almost dead." We will examine the issues of euthanasia and suicide. And we will see how people usually come to terms with their own death and the death of others close to them.

But if what these resuscitated patients tell us is true—that there is a life after death, a heaven and a hell—then the most important preparation you can make for death is not to care just for your physical needs but to be sure where you're going before you get

[3]Hebrews 9:27.

there. You are betting your own life on it. So if you're betting your life on what you now believe, you had better be right!

How can you be sure? Which of the many faiths and philosophies that attempt to deal with the meaning of death should you choose to follow? They can't *all* be true, because one often refutes the other. So which belief is right? Who's going to tell you? You can't ask the guru or minister, because he markets his faith for a living. You can't ask the man on the street, because he's no better off than you are. Who's right? Who knows?

The second part of this book will be an attempt to discover some answers to those questions. Various faiths, philosophies, and popular notions regarding the afterlife will be discussed. In a sense this search through conflicting viewpoints has been a consuming personal quest. Since I know that I'm personally *betting my life* on what I now believe, my answer to the afterlife dilemma is important to me and will become apparent as the book develops. So come with me on a personal adventure and see if you arrive at the same conclusions.

Of course, the intended purpose of this book is to help you prepare for death and the events surrounding it. My hope is that you will soon become equipped as well as possible for that inevitable journey beyond death's door. For death continues to be the most democratic of all processes—everyone participates! And everyone is given one vote. Only one! But you must vote now, before the ballot box is closed.

PART I

The Process of Dying:
What Happens?

CHAPTER II

What Does It Feel Like to Die?

Death is feared by most people. The reality of it is suppressed by some but is frighteningly foreboding to others. The reason so many of us fear death is probably because we don't have any idea of what's really going to happen when we die. And we don't know what it feels like to die.

None of us *really* believes that death will come to visit us personally. We believe it enough to buy life insurance, of course, but that's where it ends. Although some of us may say we "live for God" or for some other uplifting and esoteric purpose, we end up living for ourselves, for our own pleasures, for our own whims and desires. We do not take care to get our lives in order, for after all, death is for the fellow living next door. When we see the grim reaper visit him, we don't associate this housecall with ourselves and our own futures. *It can't happen to me*, we think, subconsciously. Our egos just will not permit it.

Yet, in the back of our minds, we do admit it. The subjects of death and dying have especially captivated collegians these days. At least 112 undergraduate courses on the subject have been identified in the United States. Surprisingly, there are now more college conferences and courses available on dying each year than there are on human sexuality.[1] The most common question raised in these conferences is "Is death oblivion?" The second most common question is "What are my chances of dying with what?"

WHAT WILL BE THE CAUSE OF YOUR DEATH?

There are three leading killers in the United States. As I discussed in my previous book, diseases of hardened arteries will kill more of us than will all other diseases put together.[2]

When Hitler appropriated all the dairy products and the "good foods" produced in occupied countries for the German people back home, this allowed occupied Norway, Sweden, Finland, and the Netherlands, the world leaders in diseases caused by hardened arteries, to experience a significant decrease in the occurrence of such health problems. Now Finland is again the leader, with the death rate from hardened arteries more than ten times greater than that in Japan, for instance. If you ask to see the coronary care units in hospitals in Japan or China, you will be told they don't have any!

It has been known for some time that "what you eat is what you get"—that is to say, the fat that hardens your arteries is about the same fat that you're now eating in your diet.

A few years ago, while giving a lecture for the American Heart Association in Helsinki, Finland, I was called by the American ambassador to investigate an outbreak of sudden unexplained deaths in the city of Joensuu that claimed the lives of young and old alike. They were

[1]Robert Hudson, "Death, Dying and the Zealous Phase," *Annals of Internal Medicine*, vol. 88, no. 696, (1978).
[2]*Beyond Death's Door* (Nashville: Thomas Nelson, 1978), p. 36.

dying from heart attacks caused by premature hardened arteries.[3] To find the reason for Finland's being the world's foremost nation with hardened arteries, a study was made of 4,000 male patients in two separate mental hospitals located in the Helsinki area. For a six-year period, Dr. Osmo Turpeinen placed one hospital on an average Finnish diet. The other hospital was given a diet low in fat (30 grams or less daily) with a high ratio of vegetable to animal fat (2:1) and a low total daily cholesterol intake (300 milligrams). The results heralded a medical breakthrough suggesting that the early phases of hardened arteries are reversible. It was found by Dr. Turpeinen that this low fat diet reduced death rates from heart attacks by one half! Deaths from all other causes, by comparison, remained unchanged, indicating a specific effect upon hardened arteries.[4]

The early "toothpaste phase," as I prefer to call it, when you can squeeze the fat out of the arteries with your thumb-nail at the autopsy table, represents this experimentally reversible phase if you reduce the blood level of cholesterol below 150 milligrams, which is well below the national average of 250 to 300 milligrams.[5] The national average is high because we're a fat nation of fat people with fat arteries on a fat diet. And the treatment of this symptomless disease is through a low-fat diet and control of predisposing diseases and not through exotic medicines or health foods.

It was once thought that high triglycerides, a

[3]Ibid., p. 40.
[4]Osmo Turpeinen, M.D., "Effect of Cholesterol-Lowering on Mortality from Coronary Heart Disease and Other Causes," *Circulation* (Jan. 1979), pp. 1–7.
[5]Richard St. Clair, "Effects of Reduced Cholesterol on Atherogenic Lesions," *Resident and Staff Physician* (June 1979), pp. 81–86.

creamy-looking fat visible in the blood, contributed directly to hardened arteries. Now it is believed that it is not really the high triglycerides but an associated deficiency of a high-density type of "good" cholesterol and too much of a low-density "bad" cholesterol that accelerates the hardening process. Bad fractions of cholesterol (blood fat) seem to occur whenever there is a dominant coronary risk factor found, such as diabetes or high blood pressure. Routine fractionation of cholesterol products is now done by most doctors and hospital laboratories to determine this ratio of "good" and "bad" cholesterol, that is, the high and low density types, to ascertain in part one's propensity to hardened arteries.

In addition to diet, certain drugs can hasten hardened arteries and, hence, the aging process. A person is about as old as his arteries. For instance, when tablets are used in place of insulin to control diabetes, there may be no protection against the hardened artery process. Other medications may actually induce disease conditions. Prolonged use of birth control tablets, for instance, is associated with a high incidence of heart attacks and premature strokes.

Contrary to public opinion, exercise does not prolong life by diminishing the incidence of heart attacks. It does, however, seem to reduce the death rate when heart attacks do occur, and joggers are known to pay fewer doctor bills than sedentary people. Conversely, however, lack of exercise accompanied by gross obesity can increase the heart attack risk rate to twice normal.

Also at variance with the opinion of most people, the most injurious of all "food additives" is merely that extra food eaten after our caloric needs have been satisfied. Overconsumption of food leads to obesity, a far greater danger to health than most all the food additives now being questioned.

Second to cardiovascular disease in frequency, cancer remains the most feared of all diseases and will afflict one in four of all Americans now living and cause ten percent of the 50 million total deaths that occur in the world each year.[6] We are constantly bombarded by messages suggesting that almost everything in our environment—external and internal—has the potential to cause cancer. However, so far there is no epidemic of cancer that can be ascribed to the introduction of the many new chemicals we've been exposed to in the past few years.[7]

The third most common cause of death is one we tend to dismiss because "it can never happen to us." According to the latest statistics, accidents account for roughly five percent of deaths in the United States yearly. Automobile accidents alone claim the lives of about 50,000 Americans each year, accounting for nearly half of all accidental deaths. Other types of fatal accidents include falls, drownings, burns and fires, and poison.

Between the ages of one and thirty-eight, the most common cause of death in America is, in fact, accidents. So, although heart disease claims more lives overall, accidents—especially automobile accidents—remain a major threat to the lives of young people.

AWAITING POSSIBLE DEATH

Most of our feelings about death relate not to the

---

[6]*American Medical News* (May 4, 1979), p. 14.
[7]W. Richard Burack, *Medical World News* (Aug. 6, 1979), p. 59.

experience itself but to the type of environment in hospitals, nursing homes, and other places where death occurs. Although the moment of death is short, the process of dying can take weeks, months, and sometimes years.

One of the main complaints of patients in intensive care wards is lack of privacy for personal needs and toiletry. Another gripe is the overly efficient attitude of well-trained nurses who don't minister to patients' fears—just to their pains. Add to this problem apathetic doctors who display no compassion for the sick, sometimes considering it a sign of weakness in themselves. A third common complaint is the separation of the patient from his family at the most critical point in his life, a time when some very personal and private interchange must take place. Unsaid things must be said.

While the emotional response—the feelings—of the patient to a strange environment can cause frightening reactions, the medical staff is usually thinking of the patient's survival and shows little concern for his emotional reaction to his illness. For instance, the blood pressure may go down, the pulse may go up, skipped heartbeats may occur, or nausea may develop. Most of these reactions aren't the direct result of the patient's illness but represent the patient's emotional response to the illness.

Meanwhile, more than half of all heart attack victims are electrically hooked up to a monitor to observe the heart for irregularities. In fact, the coronary care unit could be called a "rhythm detection center." Over eighty percent of all heart attack victims will display some irregularity of their heartbeat sometime during their hospital stay, and one-sixth of these rhythm disturbances will be fatal if they are not corrected at an early stage.

These irregular heartbeats are usually suppressed by drugs that anesthetize irritable areas of the heart in much the same way that local anesthetics "numb" the skin. For example, a Novocaine-like agent called "Lidocaine" is used to suppress irritable heartbeats. Any of the other anesthetizing drugs can be used such as Pronestyl, Norpace, Quinidine, and Bretyllium. Some of the newer drugs (one is called Inderal) work differently and antagonize the adrenalin released in response to stress by the patient's own adrenal glands.

Those Sinking Feelings

When experiencing "sinking feelings" from skipped heartbeats, often described as if an "elevator went down and left them," most patients' fear of death is easily reinforced. They may develop a sensation of impending doom. Meanwhile, only a few intensive care personnel will take time to communicate with patients and explain what medications are being given and why.

Sometimes skipped heartbeats may not be suppressible with ordinary doses of medications. However, each patient is monitored so that if the heartbeat should cease for more than a few seconds, an alarm is triggered from the TV screen in the nurses' station. When such an alarm goes off, the nurses can be subject to a sudden release of adrenalin in the stress situation and have "sinking feelings" themselves.

I recall particularly a male nurse who, in the middle of the night, was startled by such an alarm. Perceiving a fibrillation type of pattern from the patient on the tele-

35

vision screen, he developed his own skipped heartbeats in response to emergency adrenalin output. Acting on the spur of the moment, he ran into the room and noticed that the patient appeared to be unconscious. He quickly wheeled in the defibrillator machine and fired an electric current through the man's chest, making the whole body jump.

When the patient got zapped with this current, he turned over and looked the nurse in the eye. "What in the world did you do to me?"

Reconstructing the event, the chagrined nurse realized the patient had apparently turned over in his sleep and partially disconnected his electrodes, sending an alarm signal to the central nurses' station monitor by creating a false pattern of ventricular fibrillation, an emergency type of cardiac arrest that usually requires an electric shock for correction.

The nurse had forgotten the initial step used for all resuscitation efforts. We call it "shake and shout." You vigorously shake the patient and shout, "Hey, are you O.K.?"This helps to determine whether the patient is unconscious or merely in some form of semi-stupor or sleep. It helps to avoid a lot of rough treatment. (This nurse, by the way, has since become one of the finest resuscitation instructors in Georgia. He corrected the error which served as his stimulus to greater accomplishments. I would trust him with my life.)

HOW DOCTORS FEEL ABOUT DYING PATIENTS

We've mentioned the emotional needs of the seriously ill patient and how these needs are often ignored. There are also emotional needs among the medical personnel who care for acutely ill patients. We medical people try to minimize these needs, seeing them as weaknesses. We try to "keep cool" in our demeanor, but we're not always successful at this deception.

Fifty years ago, we're told, the physician would sit at the patient's bedside in an attitude of compassionate friendship. Today, the "art" of medicine has changed. Compassionate contact is sometimes limited to the laboratory results listed in the patient's chart. There is almost an attitude that the patient does not exist as a person. We seem more interested in what the figures show. The numbers are supposed to tell us what is wrong with the patient; test results sometimes replace proper examination. We are guilty, at times, of treating the laboratory and not the patient.

Where we used to be taught to diagnose by thought and deduction, we now find it more convenient to diagnose by testing. These are expensive tests that should be used to confirm a clinical diagnosis, when necessary, rather than used as "searching" tools.

With the hopeless patient, physicians are also guilty of preserving life by using elaborate treatment to maintain existence. Most doctors wouldn't want to be treated in the same fashion. They would want the purpose of their treatment directed at maintaining a *quality* of life and not primarily a *quantity* of life.

At other times we are guilty of playing "God," deciding who should receive our concentrated efforts—who should live and who should die. Did Dr. Waddell of Orange County, California, commit murder when he allowed an aborted fetus to die?[8] Do doctors have the right to judge who should live and who should be allowed to die?

[8] *60 Minutes* (CBS News Magazine Program), Sept. 16, 1979.

Not always are we so cocksure of our own infallibility, especially when something unnerving goes wrong. I recall one patient with a dangerously rapid heartbeat that we attempted to control by "overdrive" or pacing. Threading a wire through the veins, we backed it up into the heart where it could pace the heart at any rate we wished to "dial-in." The effort not only failed but seemed to make him suffer more. We tried to readjust the catheter closer to the heart wall to make the induced electrical pulse capture the patient's own heart rhythm. But we just couldn't get the thing to work right!

The more I manipulated the wire, the more angry and frustrated I became. A feeling of utter helplessness overcame me as the patient seemed to be dying in my hands, right while I was working on him. In complete despair, I said aloud, "God help me! I can't make it work!"

During these prolonged adjustments the patient soon became unconscious from progressive shock, and I started praying aloud before I even realized it: "God, make it go into the right position this time!" And it did! To my amazement and gratitude, it did! In medicine, the feeling is similar to kicking a winning field goal in the last seconds of a game. I told the patient later what had happened. Happily, he knew whom to thank, and it wasn't me!

HOW IT FEELS TO DIE

Chances are, you will die of hardened arteries. You won't feel the hardened arteries until it rather suddenly manifests itself as a heart attack or stroke or in whatever part of the body the hardened arteries are most prevalent. Consequently, it is important that we know the warning signs of an imminent heart attack, the most common result of hardened arteries, affecting one in every three of us past forty-five years of age.

However, when it comes to how we will die, most of us think of cancer first. Because of a neurotic fear of cancer, one patient with chest pain was convinced he had a lung cancer. His smoker's cough clinched the diagnosis in his own mind.

"Frankly, Doctor, I'm scared! I will be fifty in three months, the same age my father was when he died with lung cancer. I have the same aching chest pain that he described when he died."

"Have you coughed up any blood or had any weight loss?" I asked him.

"I have a cough but no blood. No weight loss."

"When does the pain get worse—when you're sitting down or when you're working?" I asked while I was examining him.

He replied, "When I'm in a hurry or sometimes when I'm working hard. It doesn't happen when I'm sitting down or doing nothing."

"What do you do to get relief from the pain?"

"Oh, it goes away in just a couple of minutes if I sit down and rest."

Just from this history alone, one could be fairly sure that he did not have cancer pains but instead "anginal" pains, which are the predecessor of heart attack. I was even more certain of this when he described the pain as a "pressure" and located it in the middle of the breastbone area and not on either side of the chest. My diagnosis was confirmed by subsequent electrocardiograms which, like his examination and his heart tones, were normal at rest but became deranged in electrocardiogram pattern when we exercised him on the treadmill to produce the same pain.

This patient's complaints are typical of those heard by doctors around the world as this silent disease of hardened arteries advances to the heart attack stage. Perhaps more than half of those in the early stages of hardened arteries will eventually experience this exertional chest pain we call *angina*.

Since our chances of succumbing to a heart attack or stroke are by far more likely than our dying as a result of any other disease, many of us have turned into exercisers, maybe playing an occasional racketball game or jogging, hoping to escape the notion that death will occur to us. In fact, right now we seem to be in excellent health. Tonight you or I will go to bed in good spirits, having eaten our usual hearty meal with gusto: perhaps a menu of the most expensive fat-marbelled steak, a baked potato smothered with butter or sour cream, topped off with our favorite high calorie, high cholesterol, ooey-gooey dessert. But consider the following experience, realizing that this is a true story that could one day be similar to your own.

> About two o'clock in the morning, I was awakened by the worst indigestion I have ever had in my life. It felt like a big stomach air bubble that had expanded to the middle of my chest, like a weight or a vise-like squeeze from a bear-hug. This crazy hurting next went into my shoulders and arms and even into my jaws. I woke my wife up with my burping. Antacids didn't help. I told her it was "bad indigestion," but she told me that I looked terrible.

WHAT DOES IT FEEL LIKE TO DIE?

She drove me to the hospital where they took an electrocardiogram, and the doctor said it was a heart attack. I was sure he had made a mistake, because I had been in perfect health all my life! It just couldn't be a heart attack! Not me!

By the time I arrived in the coronary care unit, this pressure in my chest was starting to get worse again, and they injected a syringe full of some medicines through a needle they poked into this tubing that was going into my arm. I got a little dizzy and my nose itched for a few minutes, but the pain let up. They rolled me next to a bed, cranked up the stretcher a little bit, and tumbled me off the stretcher into the bed.

By that time my wife and children had arrived at the unit.

They were told to take a seat in the waiting room. They couldn't come in to see me 'cause the visiting hours are only five minutes out of each hour in any intensive care unit. I was very frightened, but the doctors didn't seem to care. They told me down in the emergency room when I first came in that the heart attack was serious enough to kill me, and now they wouldn't even let me talk to my family. The thing that seemed to count was the medicine schedule, and if the patient just happened to make it, that was good too!

Although I felt good for some time, this pain really got bad in my chest the next morning, and I started sweating again. As I turned over in bed one of the tubes got twisted up. As I reached to untwist it my heart started skipping. Then I felt my heart stop. It actually stopped! Everything went black, and I knew then what it felt like to die! I was amazed that it was painless—like I had lost my breath, and then I wondered, *Is that all there is?*

The pain miraculously had gone! I was at peace! It felt like a "cloud nine" sensation, and the next thing I knew I sat up, got out of my body, and walked on air around the room; it was a floating sensation. I noticed that I could even walk through people! I had to walk around the nurses to see who it was they were really working on. As I looked around them, I was surprised to see myself! It was my face! And yet, here I was over here, feeling great! *That really can't be me,* I thought, *because the real me is over here!* I tried to tell them, "I'm over here. Look here." No one looked. No one seemed to hear me, and yet there were the two nurses over there, yelling out another "code 99" through the curtain.

Then I heard the code repeated over the loud speaker, and it wasn't long before two doctors came in dressed in white uniforms along with a nurse who was pushing a cart with a metal box on it, which I later learned was the "shock-box."

None of all this excitement seemed to bother me. I knew I was all right. I felt even better than ever before. But then things happened.

Next thing I knew I was leaving the room, whisking through some tunnel, tumbling head over heels at a very fast rate but without fear of falling. My body didn't bang into the sides of the walls, and I could see at the far end this small light getting bigger and bigger as I was nearing the end of the tunnel.

Upon leaving this tubular thing, I noticed how bright the whole area seemed to be; so bright yet I could still see, and it didn't blind me. It seemed as bright as the sun's rays, and yet it wasn't coming from the sun. I couldn't tell where it was coming from. I found myself in this beautiful meadow where the light made all the colors brighter. The pasture was an intense green color. It sloped slightly uphill, and there at the top I saw my parents, both my mother and father, and they appeared exactly the same as when I last saw them just before their deaths. They greeted me and loved me and put their arms around me and told me how wonderful it was to see me. I noticed other people that were dressed in bright robes as dazzling as the sun, walking around as if they had something to do.

Then we strolled arm-in-arm uphill in this meadow until we came to a rock wall. As I tried to climb over this wall, I found myself forced back into my body, back there in the hospital room. I was feeling an electric shock that ran across my chest between two big metal paddles. Some doctor had just told the nurse to "fire." I never want to feel that again. I felt like somebody hit me in the chest with a board. They seemed to be charging that metal box up again for another blow but apparently changed their minds about my form of torture, deciding to break my ribs instead. They had started pushing on my chest rhythmically when finally one of them said, "We can stop working on him now. I can get a pulse. Check his blood pressure and get some more bicarb in the I.V."

One doctor seemed to be directing the show. The pain was terrific, and my chest burned where they had put the shock paddles. I hated to come back to all of this pain when I was having such a good time in this other world.

BEFORE DEATH COMES

DEATH IS PAINLESS

What does it feel like to die? Contrary to what most people think, it doesn't hurt! Those who have experienced clinical death say it's painless—no more than a skipped heartbeat! In fact, most resuscitated patients are not afraid to die again, especially if their out-of-the-body experience was a pleasant one.

> The car was upside down, and I remember glass going around through the car like an explosion and my leg crumpling sideways under me as everything went black. Now I could see it perfectly. Other cars had stopped on the road, and I noticed that it was me in the car; my head had gone through the windshield, and they were trying to push it back through. My head's hitting the windshield must have caused the explosion of glass. Now there was a lot of blood all over the place. But I felt great! I felt so good. I thought to myself, *I must be dead for sure. But how can I be dead when I feel so good? Isn't there more to it?*

This patient later mentioned that his spirit left the scene of the accident, spun around like a whirlpool at a very rapid rate, and then entered another world. There he met his parents who had been dead for five or six years. He was overwhelmed at their appearance, which was beautiful, shiny-white, and glowing. Otherwise, they were just as he remembered them before they died. His journey with them along a rocky hillside seemed to terminate suddenly. He reentered his body just as the ambulance sped off; paramedics had been resuscitating him since arriving at the scene. Claiming this to be the most fantastic experience of his life, he said he would never be afraid of death again.

WHAT DOES IT FEEL LIKE TO DIE?

Obviously, those whose after-death experiences were not so pleasant are not so enthusiastic about their last exit from this life. However, even they now realize that the death experience itself is not painful—it's what comes afterwards that worries them now!

Strangely, people who have died do not seem to fear the moment of death again. And yet patients who have not experienced death seem to fear death the most, although none of them seem to express a fear of judgment—the one thing feared most by those who have actually been beyond death's door!

CHAPTER III

Where to Put
the Almost Dead

"I want my mama!"

That somewhat childish remark was made by an elderly patient when admitted to the hospital. This reaction was from fear of the uncertain, from the occurrence of things in a strange environment.

While blood was being withdrawn out of one arm, this patient had an intravenous solution started in the other. A double-pronged tube was placed into the nose for oxygen administration. Another tube was introduced down the throat to the stomach to keep the patient from vomiting; still another tube was inserted in the other end to prevent the person from lying in his own urine.

I guess I would want my mama, too!

More than eighteen million Americans are over the age of sixty-five, and only two million Americans die each year. Retired members of our society will soon outnumber working members. This shift has also resulted in eighteen percent of all deaths occurring in nursing homes or hospitals instead of in the private home setting, where, in years past, the dying person was able to be with his family.

Hence, the death event has been transferred from the

home to an institutional setting where the medical staff is not trained or equipped to care for the emotional needs of this distinctive patient. Let me reemphasize: We physicians have had *no* formal training in the needs of the dying patient, nor have most nurses, ministers, and social workers.

This shift of death to an institutional setting reflects our unwillingness to express our gratitude to the elderly with loving care. We don't want the responsibility or the work it entails. While we are aware of child abuse, we are not as cognizant of abuse of the elderly and the degree with which it is occurring. Family members are increasingly abusing their elderly relatives. Some abuses are less obvious and are in the form of inadequate attention or purposeful neglect. Other examples are more flagrant. There have been reports of elderly parents being given large doses of tranquilizers to make them more "manageable" while the children go out to the store or to do other errands. Sometimes parents have been tied up; others are made to change their will under psychological threats, according to Dr. Suzanne Steinmetz, researcher in domestic violence at the University of Delaware. She has testified on elderly abuse to the House Committee on Science and Technology.[1]

Just the other day I asked to see the family of a charity patient assigned to me in one of the hospitals. The patient said she hadn't seen her family in two weeks. Then I learned that a neighbor had originally found this woman lying in bed in her own excrement. The patient had apparently been left alone at home by her grown

[1]*Geriatrics* (May 1979), p. 23.

children for four or five days and was unable to move because of her illness. Bed sores had already developed underneath the fecal material. Her children apparently didn't care, and when the nurse tried to call them, they couldn't be found. Child abuse is no worse than abuse of the elderly, and it happens all the time.

For various ignoble reasons, many families want Granny in the grave. Useless and in the way around the house, exhibiting loss of memory, irritable and more demanding, wetting herself, evacuating in her underpants, she has become a nuisance.

One family, for example, has already talked things over, and all have agreed that Granny should have no medical measures used to "bring her back." So when she eventually comes down, say, with pneumonia or some other incidental illness that is potentially curable, the family promptly will throw in the towel as if it were a terminal catastrophe. Some will demand that "nothing be done to prolong her." Some will be blatantly disappointed when they learn that she'll soon recover.

Not too long ago, I saw a woman lying at the foot of a stairway at an apartment building where many elderly and retired people live. She was comatose and paralyzed on one side. One of her eyes was blackened. I called an ambulance and went with her to the hospital.

The family, having been notified by neighbors, converged on the hospital, and we met in the emergency room. I got the same feedback from all of them: "If Granny looks bad, don't try to save her. She told us that she didn't want to live."

This patient hadn't fallen down the stairs because of a stroke but had merely lost her balance and fractured her skull in the fall. A subdural hematoma (clot on the surface of the brain) developed underneath the fracture site. A few hours later, a neurosurgeon removed the clot, after which she promptly recovered. No more paralysis and no more coma.

To the family's consternation, she is still living today. Strangely enough, she has also recovered much of her memory and functions while convalescing in the nursing home. Today she is ready to be released to her own home, and I wonder what will happen when I break this "good news" to the family.

The point is, I almost succumbed to the pressures brought to bear by the family, who were content to see Granny in the grave. Even if our medical practice is primarily centered upon the patient, it still can be strongly influenced by family pressures. If families become, shall we say, overly zealous in their abandonment of older family members, this can subtly influence doctors' decisions. It may subconsciously dictate them. In the popular demand for "dignified dying," we physicians will have to guard against contributing to Granny's premature death.

The two institutions that are most prominent in dealing with death are hospitals and nursing homes. But a third—the hospice—has developed as an alternative that allows continued interaction between the patient and his family and friends.

HOSPITALS: EFFICIENT DISPASSION

The hospital environment is completely depersonalized; medical personnel ask the families of patients to leave or to go to the waiting room so that doctors and nurses can efficiently and dispassionately perform routine duties. Moreover, the sicker the patient becomes, the more we doctors seem to subject him to needles, catheters, ventilators, and other unpleasant gadgetry. As his condition deteriorates, the more frightened and lonely he becomes. Hurting, nauseated, bewildered, and dazed, the dying patient is deprived of his friends, his family, and his security.

When the actual death scene is finally acted out, it usually occurs in an intensive care unit, in a completely formal atmosphere of medical routine. The death process is enacted among white uniforms, bloody bedsheets, and complicated gadgetry, an environment as morose as the morgue itself. The five-minute visiting time allowed out of each hour for the family is cancelled as the death process approaches. Resuscitative means of retrieval are sometimes pursued for hours—unnecessarily. We are frequently guilty of persisting even when the situation is obviously lost, in the name of science, of course. When prolonged attempts at cures are at last abandoned, many doctors desert the dying, leaving the patient insecure at the most frightening stage of his illness.

When will this trend end? Only when we develop in our hospital staffs the conviction that compassion should replace scientific efficiency when death is inevitable. It will end only when we physicians allow ourselves to empathize with patients, when we have the courage to obliterate all discomfort with abundant medication, when we learn not only *how* to treat but *when* to treat, and when we realize the dignity of every individual, each made in God's own image.

The first law of medicine, which should remain our

guide, is *primum non nocere,* which means "if you can't do any good, at least do no harm."

NURSING HOMES: THE WAITING PLACE

Unfortunately, the most common alternative to a modern, cold, efficient hospital is a weary, drab, and dilapidated old nursing home. Life expectancy reached a record high in 1977 of 73.2 years, and it keeps increasing, as does the number of elderly people and nursing homes.

Nursing homes are now a measure of the change in America's cultural heritage. By the rest of the world's standards, we are considered "rich" because we have running water, are able to throw things away, and can afford to place our parents in a home for the elderly. The trend for the modern family is to divest itself of the unwanted elderly. Some nursing homes represent receptacles for what some consider human "junk." But things have slowly improved. The deprived souls and near-zombies who used to walk and sleep in rat-infested firetraps have seen their living conditions improved as stringent regulations have been enforced.

"How do you like your nursing home?" I asked Mrs. Molly Shelborn, a new resident at one particular home.

She replied, "If you call this a home, you're wrong. The people I live with are old, and a lot of them don't know where they are or what they're doing."

Mrs. Shelborn was in a wheelchair, recovering from what had been a hopeless loss of memory, recurrent epileptiform seizures, and a severe debilitating weakness. This had all been secondary to an underlying pernicious anemia that had been undiagnosed for months.

As soon as the anemia was correctly treated, all the seizures stopped and the previous sedating medications for convulsions were no longer needed. She woke up, became aware of her surroundings, and got out of her wheelchair! She gradually regained strength, was dismissed from the nursing home, and now—instead of being a helpless invalid—travels extensively. She goes where she wants to go and does what she wants to do.

I often wonder how many other people are in nursing homes, disabled from undiagnosed, remediable conditions.

Further down the hall in the same nursing home, I met another old friend, an elderly gentleman in his eighties who had had several cardiac arrests about ten years previously. We had thought of abandoning the hopeless task of multiple resuscitations at that time— but he finally recovered! He's still living today and always has a story to tell me.

You know, I still remember that time you worked on me on the floor. Even though I didn't have any experience after I died, I am still sure glad you brought me back. I still have a lot of fun even though I can't get around too much. I talk a lot with the other patients and with the people who work here.

I used to think that living was for any bang you could get out of life—mostly sex, I suppose. Then, as people grew older, I noticed they seemed to get more interested in food. In this nursing home environment, where the people are still older, it seems that they are not as interested in food—instead, they seem to be living for the next bowel movement!

Every day this challenge seems to become their greatest accomplishment!

I guess my greatest goal every day is reading this old book with the wrinkled pages that my father gave to me. (He was holding up his tattered old Bible.) You know, when I died back there, I found out how to live. This book gave me the answers I had been searching for all of my life. I never realized it was right under my nose all the time in this dusty old book, lying back on the shelf in my bedroom closet. Now I know you don't have to die to learn how to live. I thank God I am still living to find it out!

These moving words from this wise old man brought to mind a question I had asked myself in the past. If I get to be his age, will the "golden years" truly be golden? Will the younger generations be eager to sit at *my* feet and listen to *me* impart the wealth of knowledge and wisdom I have gained from years of experience and maturity? Or am I fooling myself? Will no one show up? Maybe just my doctor will stop by the home, or perhaps just my children.

HOSPICES: DEATH'S MIRROR

Widespread interest in the "hospice care concept" is a comparatively recent phenomenon in the United States. However, this concept of care for the terminally ill has long been practiced in Europe.

The term *hospice* comes from a medieval word meaning a "place of shelter," specifically for travelers on a difficult journey. The current use of the term describes institutions designed specifically for the control and relief of the emotional and physical suffering of terminally ill patients. The idea comes from Britain where many hospices have been established in the last ten years, most notably St. Christopher's Hospice in Sydenham, a suburb of London.

Since the establishment of St. Christopher's Hospice, many similar institutions have arisen in other countries, including the Royal Victoria Hospital in Montreal, hospices in New Haven and Marion counties of California, St. Luke's Hospital in New York, and St. Thomas Hospital in London. Such hospices actually serve as a combination home and hospital. The patient's family come and go as they please, thus furnishing the patient with companionship. The medical personnel are always available to see the patient.

It's always been a problem to find members of the family who are willing and able to give medical treatment, such as narcotic injections, in the home. This becomes a necessity when the patient becomes too ill to swallow pain medications. At those times when "shots" are imperative for comfort, we are frequently forced to place the patient either in a hospital where daily expenses may exceed one hundred dollars or in a nursing home where daily expenses exceed twenty-five dollars (and more with today's inflation). All this just to give shots, which are less than five dollars per day.

Why not have the patient remain in his home and have the medical personnel attend him there? If the family is willing to learn to administer the injections and stay on top of any pain development, this will take care of most of his nursing needs; but most families don't want to learn—especially when they can get Medicare to pay for hospitalization. Private duty nurses, another option, can be more expensive than the cost of being in the hospital.

Thus, the concept of bringing the hospital to the home is the purpose of the hospice. It offers domiciliary care since the family can live in with the patient. It's a place where the nurse is continually available, and the doctor is on call for the patient's needs. The hospice may also serve as a headquarters for those who are able to remain at home under the care of a family member trained to give medications.

Proponents of the hospice concept maintain that "wherever possible, a dying patient should be allowed to finish his life at home, surrounded by concerned family, among his own possessions, and in a setting that can maximize psycho-social comfort."[2] A recent editorial relates man to animal: "The urge to remain in one's lair during moments of crisis is innate."[3] Perhaps this animal instinct explains in part why so many wish to die at home. Should we not honor this instinct?

However, a complex of social, familial, and residential changes in the past several decades militates against home-dying. The current change of a physician's headquarters from home to hospital, with the resultant decrease in house calls, has tended to move the care of the seriously ill or dying from the home to either the hospital or nursing home. Many problems were once resolved in the home, but doctors no longer make house calls, at least not in the big cities.

[2]Melvin J. Krant, "The Hospice Movement," *The New England Journal of Medicine*, vol. 299, no. 10 (Sept. 7, 1978), pp. 546–49.
[3]J.R. Coll, "Dying at Home," *General Practitioner*, vol. 28 (1978), pp. 3–4.

Although some home care of the dying still exists, frightening or upsetting symptoms can occur any time of the day or night, leaving the patient and family feeling anxious and helpless at such moments. Here again, the hospice concept is attractive since medical help is available on a twenty-four-hour basis.

Another misconception in medical circles is that constant pain requires constant attention and treatment. Analgesics should be given routinely in painful diseases so that the patient does not have to ask for them out of exacerbation caused by pain. The letters "p.r.n." are added all too frequently to a patient's chart; this means the patient must ask for pain relief medications before they are given. Feelings of isolation and hopelessness are bad enough without having to endure pain unnecessarily. Frequently this weariness leads to depression and sometimes is projected outwardly as hostility and resentment toward family and medical attendants. The patient can find no meaning in all of this suffering—so why let him suffer? In a hospice or at home, a large number of volunteers can assist the family in alleviating the patient's hopelessness. Here the minister can approach the patient at any time, day or night, with the greatest reassurance of all to the dying patient—the Scriptures and their promises of another life.

It is because of these advantages that the concept of the hospice has become popular. This dwelling place, a modified hospital-home, permits patients who are aware that they are dying with some progressive disease to have the benefits of skilled nursing care and an assortment of medications tailored to the patient's needs. This is combined with the personal contact of family and friends who wish to share the last few days with the patient and to have personal communication with him or her during life's most important adventure, the journey beyond death's door.

The family should learn to sit quietly with the dying, to keep him in touch with life as much as possible and to see to his continuous care until the end. They should learn to perform tasks, such as feeding the patient, with patience and devotion; some form of communication with the patient who cannot speak should be maintained. Psychological support of the dying patient through evaluation and expression of normal and appropriate emotional responses to his own sorrow and anticipations are an integral part of the program. Before the emotional and psychological needs of a patient can be adequately met, someone must attend to the practical concerns of the patient, including wet bedsheets, physical discomfort, insomnia, and all aspects of patient comfort.

As the hospice concept grows through the establishment of new facilities in the United States, care must be taken in the architecture not to make the hospice a "death house" for the dying patient. Bright colors and a cheerful atmosphere, conveniences of toiletry and sleep-in beds for close members of the family, and a call system for medications or medical assistance as necessary should all be available.[4]

Times When the Hospice Is Not the Answer

With the great advances made in the diagnosis and

[4]William M. Markel and Virginia B. Sinon, "Abstracts from the Hospice Concept," *A Cancer Journal for Clinicians*, vol. 28, no. 4 (July-Aug. 1978), p. 225.

treatment of disease, we medical people too often consider the patient as a collection of symptoms and signs rather than as a human being representing a member of a family. We become so intent on preserving life that we sometimes make death more unpleasant than it already is. However, the physician can make the wrong diagnosis and become so bent upon the prognosis that the patient is hopelessly sentenced to death. Although rare indeed, I must give you an example or two of mistakes that could have been made.

There was a fifty-six-year-old woman who had had a radical mastectomy three years previously. She developed shortness of breath, which was interpreted as "cancer spread to the lungs," and an enlarged liver which was interpreted as "another locus of cancer spread." Finally she went into a semi-stupor, which suggested brain involvement from the same spreading cancer. Instead of cancer, all of these findings were due to an advancing heart failure, which was causing congestion of the lungs, liver, and brain; all of these organs returned to normal when treatment for the heart failure was instituted. This patient would otherwise have been allowed to die needlessly.

Another case, recounted by Dr. Irwin Krakoff, director of the Cancer Center at the University of Vermont, was a fifty-four-year-old man whose X rays showed white nodules in the lung root areas, typical of cancer of the lung. Shortly thereafter he began developing bone pains in the right shin area. A bone scan showed a defect in the bone consistent with cancer, probably spread from the lung. A "CAT" scan of the brain showed three other defects that looked like the same cancer.

When the shin bone was examined, when the nodules in the brain were biopsied, and when the lungs were investigated, all of these areas were found to be abscesses, not cancers. These infected areas responded to antibiotic treatment; the patient recovered, was discharged, and is now living and well. If the doctors assumed, without looking, that the patient had cancer, he now would be dead and six feet under.[5]

Still another case was that of a fifty-nine-year-old woman with a lump in the right breast and a fracture of the left arm that occurred without apparent reason. The fracture was thought to be related to cancer near or in the bone. However, removal of the breast lump showed a noncancerous adenoma and the parathyroid gland was found to have a small nodule producing chemical substances that had caused bone degeneration sufficient to create the fracture. No cancer!

The point of all of this is to underscore the importance of proper medical examination and biopsy to confirm all diagnoses before instigating treatment or relegating someone as a terminal patient to the nursing home or hospice.

When we are satisfied that incurability is present, and when we know the patient is dying, then the hospital offers no advantages other than comforting medications. The patient can be treated at home or in a hospice. At the same time there could be a shift of treatment objectives toward the patient's comfort and not his survival. Why can't pain medications be given at home or in a hospice on a basis that anticipates the

---

[5]Dr. Irwin H. Krakoff, "Opinions," *A Cancer Journal for Clinicians*, vol. 29, no. 2 (Mar.–April 1979), pp. 109–10.

pain? The doses can be increased to avoid pain, nausea, and fear as the patient progresses toward death. After settling his financial, personal, and spiritual affairs—after making himself right with God—the dying person can face death without undue apprehension and with some form of dignity.

In summary, the hospice concept has the following purposes:

- To keep the patient home as long as possible.
- To educate health professionals and lay people.
- To supplement existing services.
- To support the family as the unit of care.
- To help the patient to live as fully as possible.
- To keep costs down.
- To allow for the spiritual preparation of the patient for the next life.

The criteria for admission should include these conditions:

- Prognosis must be for death in either a few weeks or a few months.
- Referring physician must agree to continue his association with the patient.
- Spouse or family member or friend must be ready to assume responsibility for primary care (the medical staff gives secondary and symptomatic care only).
- Patient must live within a thirty-mile radius of the hospice so that the family can provide care on a rotation basis.
- There must be proof of diagnosis, an advanced

state of the disease, and prior treatment reaching the stage of ineffectiveness.

For a complete list of hospices in the United States, see the Appendix.

FINAL WORDS ABOUT THE TERMINALLY ILL

Sometimes the psychological and economic problems confronting the terminally ill patient are more distressing than the disease itself. There are urgent, practical questions such as "How long will it be?" "How hard will it be on my family?" "Will the money last?"

Depression and anxiety plague the relatives of the terminally ill patient as well as the patient himself. Unfinished business, financial problems of support, plans and dreams now destroyed, the unexpected changes— all these are legitimate sources of concern and emotional distress. Family members also have many questions: "How much does he know?" "How should I tell the children?" "What do I do if he gets in trouble in the middle of the night?" "How will I manage alone after my loved one is gone?"

These concerns, as well as physical relief, must also be considered in the treatment plan. Unlike acute illness where recovery is expected, in terminal illness every member of the family is affected. Adjustment to life without the patient begins before death, and this adjustment is difficult and often requires professional treatment and guidance.

Active participation by family members is part of the process of separation, and it has been observed clinically that those who are actively involved in the process of care while the patient is still alive are less prone to guilt and self-criticism after the death of the individual.[6] Guilt involves the "uninvolved."

LET'S LEARN TO RESPECT OUR ELDERS

When one is old—and therefore more experienced and knowledgeable—why is he often *less* respected? The truth is, elderly people in our culture are disregarded, shunned, or discarded like worn-out garments. As the unwanted generation, the elderly are coming to see that age is an insult. Rejected and cast out of the mainstream of life, they are herded into a lonely Siberian existence.

A patient of mine once complained,

All my troubles began when I reached sixty-five. You had to retire whether you wanted to or not in the company I worked for. I was a good machinist and their best crane operator.

Within a year after I retired, I found I wasn't keeping in good shape. I had promised myself I would do gardening, jogging, and bicycling. Then I started putting on a little weight and that's when I had my heart attack. I felt fine one day, and the next day, bingo! . . . I was in trouble. Then I had a second heart attack two years later, and after that I got so short of breath I couldn't even walk to the mailbox in front of my house. My wife had died, and since I had trouble taking care of myself, the kids insisted that I come to this nursing home. And here I am.

Even though I can't do any physical activity, my mind is as sharp as it ever was, and I could teach a lot

---

[6]J. Craven and F. S. Wald, "Hospice Care for Dying Patients," *American Journal of Nursing*, vol. 75 (1975), pp. 1816–22.

of these kids a useful trade in machining and welding if they would only ask me. I disagree that just because people are old, they are worthless. They don't belong to the scrap heap. A lot of us have something to contribute if they'd only let us.

Surprising to me, I have found my attitude changing. I had always regarded the elderly as "elderly," but now that life expectancy has increased for the average person, it occurred to me that each of us is becoming one of the "elderly" every day. Every day each one of us is older. And as we get older, the years seem to go by faster!

Now I am trying to take advantage of opportunities to enjoy my elderly patients. They have a wealth of knowledge, and if I don't learn from them now, tomorrow may be too late.

CHAPTER IV
Is Killing Ever Merciful?

Who should "pull the plug?" Some patients become dependent upon artificial means of continued survival such as heart pumps, kidney machines, mechanical respirators, and drugs to support blood pressure. Although the patient will not live forever on these artificial devices, he can live long enough to run up tens of thousands of dollars in hospital bills. Who's going to decide when these bills should end? Are we preserving life or simply prolonging death?

I cannot hope to comment exhaustively on a topic as complex as euthanasia, or "mercy killing." However, we need to be aware of current trends and practices— practices that will affect us when we become "the dying patient."

EUTHANASIA—WHAT IS IT?

Euthanasia is the purposeful termination of a patient's life by any direct means, as for instance, an overdose of narcotics. Euthanasia is the deliberate killing of a patient.

There was recently the case of a well-known physician who voluntarily gave up his license and moved to another state before the medical board of New Jersey could review charges against him that might have led to his permanent license revocation. His move was caused by the death of a sixty-four-year-old terminal cancer patient who had asked the physician to hasten his death. The patient's spouse told the medical reviewing board that she approved of the physician's action. The doctor reportedly had administered morphine, phenobarbital, and insulin. The patient was not diabetic and died twenty-four hours later. This is direct euthanasia. The physician was censured by his own medical staff, and the hospital later asked for his resignation.

During routine rounds at one of our larger hospitals we found evidence of indirect attempts at euthanasia by meddling visitors or hospital personnel. An IV drip-rate had been mysteriously increased from 50 to 200 cubic centimeters per hour in one patient who had advanced heart failure. This happened on three occasions. A ventilator had been disconnected on two occasions from another terminal patient with chronic lung disease. Both patients' maintenance lifelines had been secretly rearranged.

Some also consider euthanasia to be intentional omission or discontinuance of artificial life support mechanisms or otherwise the purposeful avoidance of intervention when emergency situations develop.

Let me emphasize that the hospice concept discussed in the last chapter does not support euthanasia in any form, as some opponents of the hospice movement fear. At a hospice, medications are given for the direct comfort of the patient, and overdoses are never given. Instead of terminating the patient's life, there is an exercise of humaneness; life and death decisions are made to the patient's benefit. Terminal care is much more comprehensive in its objective methods than the elected procedure of euthanasia.

Euthanasia involves exterminating patients rather than allowing them to die naturally. To me, there is a vast difference between giving a patient an overdose and making the decision not to attach a patient to a ventilator because it would not improve his or her condition.

When a family understands that the physician will devote all of his efforts to treating the patient exactly as he would want to be treated under the same circumstances, then situations of useless prolongation of life, rising hospital bills, and unnecessary suffering of both family and patient can be avoided. To be precise, one should remember that when cancer invades the patient, it also invades the family; the "plug" often should never be "put in" in the first place. After a terminal condition is evaluated, the physician may write "no code" upon the chart so that resuscitative measures are avoided by all hospital personnel on the other shifts. This way everyone is aware of the decision. At the same time, orders can be written to read, "no ventilators" or "no supportive measures except for comfort." Such orders can avoid the predicament of a cruel and unnecessary existence brought on by use of ultramodern equipment. Death will occur from the natural causes of the disease itself. Thus, all of the heartaches of the "living vegetable" can usually be avoided by simple discussion with the family before any supportive measures become necessary.

Consider this next case. A despondent twenty-one-year-old girl took 140 tranquilizers and attempted to drive her car into a stone wall. Hospitalized in a coma in Denville, New Jersey, she remained comatose and, except for her heartbeat, was lifeless, staring without sight, recognizing no one, tube fed, and exhibiting decerebrate findings indicating irreparable, total brain damage.

When the parents asked for the respirator to be removed, the doctor was reticent and refused. Eventually the case came to court, and many witnesses from different theological, medical, and legal points of view were obtained; finally the court ordered that the respirator be removed while she was still alive. Contrary to expectations, Karen Ann Quinlan continued to live, breathing on her own, and later was sent to a nursing home. Did "pulling the plug" in this case constitute a euthanasia attempt?

In Chattanooga there was a similar case when a thoracic surgeon refused to terminate a ventilator, which kept the patient surviving in spite of an incurable illness. The family asked that all life-support measures be terminated. The doctor said "no." The case was taken to court. However, the patient eventually died despite continued supportive measures, and I suspect the surviving family is now faced with horrendous hospital bills and unpleasant memories.

What do churches have to say about the terminal patient? The Catholic tradition does not recognize an absolute moral obligation to use "extraordinary" means of preserving life. "Extraordinary" is defined as "all medicines, treatments and operations, which cannot be obtained or used without excessive expense, pain, or other inconvenience or which, if used, would not offer a reasonable hope of benefit."[1] The Jewish opinion, on the other hand, is expressed as a consensus among orthodox, conservative, and reformed rabbinic authorities: ". . . although active euthanasia is forbidden, passive euthanasia in certain circumstances is permitted by Jewish law. One is permitted, but not obliged, to remove any artificial means keeping the terminal patient alive because such activity is not considered a positive action."[2] There are several supporters of this same position in Protestantism.[3]

THE RIGHT TO DIE

Do patients have the "right to die"? Many patients think so and are arranging "living wills," addressed to "my family, clergyman, physician and lawyer, for a time when I may be incapable of deciding my own future." The usual will is simple and contains one paragraph:

> If there is no reasonable expectation of my recovering from an illness or injury, I request that I be allowed to die in dignity and not be kept alive by heroic measures. I ask that drugs be administered to me only for the relief of pain and not to prolong my earthly life, even if these pain-killing drugs may hasten my death.

[1]G. Kelly, "The Duty to Preserve Life," *Theological Studies,* vol. 22, no. 228 (1961).
[2]B. L. Sherwin, "Jewish Views on Euthanasia," *The Humanist,* vol. 34, no. 19 (1974).
[3]P. Ramsey, "The Patient as a Person," *New Haven and London* (New Haven, Conn.: Yale University Press, 1970), p. 113.

Again the question is, does omission of life-support measures constitute euthanasia? In some cases, perhaps it does. But if, indeed, the patient has no "reasonable expectation" of recovery, the doctor may decide that extraordinary measures should be avoided.

SUICIDE—PULLING YOUR OWN PLUG

Mr. Rubinstein was a patient who had been a widower for four years. A literary genius, he was a connoisseur of the classics. Although he had some visitors among both his close friends and his old cronies, I noted he never invited the rabbi to visit him.

One day I asked him, "Since you know that you are dying, why don't you turn to God for guidance and help?"

He replied, "I don't have any use for that. I left the synagogue and all the faith it represents when I was in childhood. I may be a Jew by birth but not by religion."

He continued, "But there is something you can do for me, Doctor! Let me have a bottle of sleeping pills. You can do it—so I won't have to go through the agony of pain and watch myself as I wither away. Then my friends will remember me the way they see me now. If you can't get me the sleeping pills, get me a revolver and leave it in my bedside drawer when no one is watching you. Otherwise I could decide to jump out of the window or do something else!"

At first I thought he was joking, but I soon got the message. It was one of frank premeditation.

Here was a patient, apparently of sane mind, who intended to take his own life. Wouldn't voluntary euthanasia, another name for suicide, be a good thing in such cases? No! Making voluntary euthanasia lawful would put a damper on the patient's will to live and eventually serve as an excuse to abrogate our responsibility to the frail and weak, the disabled and the dying. The thought that a quick release should be legalized should introduce another thought: Human nature, being what it is, would not allow euthanasia to remain voluntary for very long!

Also, think of the times when you've been in pain. A death wish at such times is not uncommon, but aren't you glad those caring for you didn't take your wish seriously?

It has been reported that eighty-five percent of those resuscitated after suicide attempts are actually glad to be alive! The after-death experiences of attempted suicides that I have been able to collect have always been hellish. I have never heard a person who has attempted suicide describe a good experience. Their suicide enactment was really a cry for help. So also are many of the cries for relief from fear or pain or from the dreaded outcome of a depressing life.

As it turned out, Mr. Rubinstein also needed more time to cope with thoughts of dying and to find out what was right for him. He had made a decision for his own death needlessly, because ten days later he was out of the hospital! Chemotherapy had caused regression of his malignancy so that he lived comfortably for another nine months. Thereafter he found it easier to live a day at a time, not asking for absolution from his dilemma but instead looking for the right way to use the time he had left.

I remember a physician's mother who had been distraught ever since the unexpected death of her husband from, of all things, a hemorrhoidectomy! He bled to death. He was in his late thirties. I had treated him for coronary heart disease and arthritis. When he was sent home following a routine hemorrhoid operation, he suddenly started losing large amounts of blood. Before his surgeon could replace the blood by emergency transfusions, he succumbed to an intervening heart attack precipitated by the severe anemia caused by the blood loss.

Despondent since that time, the widow tried to take her life with an overdose of barbiturates. Her stomach was pumped, antidotes were given, fluids forced, and she was able to excrete most of this lethal load of barbiturates through the kidneys without the necessity of peritoneal dialysis or other heroic measures.

Did she have a right to die? She thought so. Some years later, when she became breathless from her own smoker's bronchitis, she tried it again. This time it worked. Although she had eliminated herself, the problems of her children, now without parents, became progressively worse.

The Bible includes admonitions concerning suicide. It states that the fullness of our time is in God's hands.[4] The Bible forbids murder, even against oneself.[5] Furthermore, it says our lives are not our own: They are God's.[6]

EUTHANASIA IN PERSPECTIVE

Euthanasia takes many forms and many meanings. There exists today the "Euthanasia Society of America"

[4]Psalm 31:15.
[5]Exodus 20:13; 1 Corinthians 6:18–20.
[6]1 Corinthians 6:19; Genesis 9:5,6.

formed in 1935 by the Unitarian minister, Charles Francis Potter. Its purpose is to promote the acceptability of mercy killing for the terminally ill who are in great pain or for the permanently helpless who exhibit great physical or mental incapacity.

However, most leading physicians in our society and in the world oppose any law that would give the medical profession a sanction to intervene and terminate life. However, physicians have the same gamut of personality variations found in society at large. Some are hot, and some are cold. Some are really smart, and some are not so smart. Some have compassion, and some are calloused.

One doctor I talked to said, "I believe every patient has the right to take his own life. After all, it is your own life, and if you are in your right mind, you have a right to dispose of it if you so wish."

Fortunately, all doctors don't feel this way. This particular physician also felt at liberty to give sedatives to dying patients who are potentially suicidal: "Some doctors are afraid to give their dying patients sedatives—what are they afraid of? That the patient is going to kill himself? Well, isn't that decision his right? So, if my patient asks me for sleeping tablets, I will give him, let's say, thirty, forty, fifty Nembutals and tell him 'one a night for sleep.' But the patient really knows what I mean: He could take them all at once if he wanted to."

Sometimes a physician is not adamant in taking a stand for or against survival. In fact, he may take no stand at all, neither with the family nor with the medical personnel under his jurisdiction. He may instead allow the responsibility to be passed on to the house staff by writing such vague orders as "do everything except intubate" (meaning do not attach to a ventilator) or an order such as "shock him once" (meaning that if he doesn't respond immediately to defibrillation you quit trying).

If resuscitation efforts are to be limited, such orders should be specific and made by the primary physician with the family's informed consent. Such procedure will usually suffice if the family is aware that there is no hope—and if the physician tells them he will make sure that the patient feels no pain, no anxiety, no fear, and that he will personally take care of the patient as if he were in his own family. Efforts to insure the patient's greatest possible comfort requires finesse and foresight. To allow a conscious patient to die horribly—with pain, smothering, fear, or loneliness—is no longer necessary nor tolerable.

It is fashionable in this age of man-centeredness and humanism for people to take charge of human destiny: the physician over his patient; the despondent over himself. The fact of the matter is, we are not our own property. By creation and by redemption, God says we belong to Him. We are His property. Thus, let us stand against the taking of one another's lives *and* against the taking of our own.

CHAPTER V

A Realistic Look at Dying

The dying patient is often the first to realize that his death is inevitable—perhaps even before his physician becomes aware of it. When the verdict becomes apparent, the patient's friends and family, now more needed than ever, often abandon him because they are too afraid to talk to him. This patient—the dying patient—becomes the most neglected of all patients. Members of the family pretend that death is not occurring, both in conversations with the patient and with each other. They often continue to play these games until it's too late. Disinterested physicians and untrained ministers also don't seem to know what to do. Most seminaries and medical schools have no practical training for their students in the care of the dying patient and how to meet his emotional needs.

The dying patient is treated as if he had some social disease, as if he is an outcast. Yet, he represents a captive audience. Rarely before has he been interested in the possibility of life after death or in the most available reference source for the subject, the Bible. Now that he must face death, he wants all the details he can get. First, he wants to know how painful death will be. Then he may ask, "Is there life after death? Is there really a heaven and a hell? Is it really safe to die?"

A REALISTIC LOOK AT DYING

To best understand what a dying person goes through, imagine *you* are the patient. There you are, lying in bed, a little woozy from the last injection you had for pain. That pain, let's say, is from deep bone aches where cancer is enlarging and eroding the bone, having spread there from some other place. Not all of your pain is relieved. You are still able to think, and you hear your family talking in quiet whispers outside your hospital room. Apparently they don't want to upset you while they discuss the gravity of your condition and what should be done about it.

Finally, they enter the room with forced smiles and "chin-up" attitudes, full of oozing condolences and false encouragement and faking an attitude that you will recover, when you've already been told by the doctors that your condition is fatal!

You indirectly ask them what it must feel like to die, but they either change the subject or find an excuse for their early departure. When you ask them about God or suggest they discuss the Bible, they avoid the subject, saying that the minister is coming to discuss these things with you. They want to know if there is anything they can do for you, but they really don't want to be bothered with anything beyond your physical needs. They mention that the children are doing fine, how everyone misses you, and so on.

The minister finally arrives, his Bible in hand. He reads a few verses to you, says a prayer, and then reminds you to "keep doing what the doctor tells you." When you ask him about life after death, he says, "Oh, yes, God says there is life after death." But he will proceed to avoid specifically answering your questions concerning death itself and the next life. You get the impression that *he doesn't want to confirm that you are dying;* discussing death is actually disturbing to him. As it does with other people, your condition surfaces within your minister the dreaded realization of his own vulnerability and mortality. There are, of course, pastors remaining who will discuss death and the afterlife with dying patients.

Then the doctor comes in, making his daily rounds, followed by a nurse. With chart in hand, he asks you, "How are you feeling today?" Perhaps he's really interested in reading the chart and isn't particularly listening to your answer.

When you inquire, "How much longer do I have?" he more often than not responds, "I don't know; your disease could be suppressed for a long time with the chemicals you're receiving in your veins each day."

Since the doctor appears to be avoiding many of your questions, this gives you the courage to ask him another: "Do you believe in life after death?" He may smile benignly at this foolish question, mumble something, and walk out, still reading your chart.

Who do you think is the most neglected patient in the whole hospital? You are! People treat you like you've got something contagious. You represent a problem that is personally too painful for them to handle, and they try to avoid you as a result.

I say all this to motivate those of you who are well to reach out to the dying. They want to hear from you. Many of your own insecurities will be conquered as you concentrate on meeting the patient's needs.

If you decide to take this challenge, you can probably learn of someone who would appreciate your visits from your pastor, doctor, or hospital or nursing home personnel. In your initial contact with any patient, you can simply state why you are visiting him or her. Mention who sent you. Offer to do trivial errands. You might eventually ask the patient what the doctors have found wrong with him. This way you will soon find out how much the patient knows about himself: whether he has cancer, uremia, leukemia, or some other terminal illness. Perhaps you will already know the diagnosis, but you may want to find out if the patient is apprised of this finding. The answers will tell you how openly you can talk about the matter of death.

Try to make your subsequent visits at a time when the patient will be alone, with no third person to divert the conversation. When alone, the patient more often will open the door to frank discussions, posing problems directly related to the outcome of his illness. Nevertheless, *you should wait for his invitation to discuss these subjects.* If the conversation turns to a discussion of the meaning of death, feel free to tell what resuscitated patients have reported: what they felt, what they saw, and how escaping death affected their lives. These conversations will eventually lead to the source of all answers about death, the Scriptures themselves.

A frank question for anyone, sick or well, when the circumstances are appropriate, would be, "What do you think will happen to you when you die?" Don't tell him! Ask him! Supply the questions; God will supply the answers.

STAGES OF DYING

The stages through which a dying person passes were outlined in my first book, with acknowledgment made to Elisabeth Kubler-Ross, author of *On Death and*

Dying. I want to present these stages again, this time labelling each stage with a word that begins with "R" for better memory recall. Bear in mind as you review these stages that they are not always sequential for the patient, nor does the dying person necessarily go through all the stages.

1. *Rejection.* The first stage of death is almost always rejection, rejection of the catastrophic announcement of doom. When the doctor implies that death may occur, the usual response is "Doctor, you have the wrong patient," or, "You've got the wrong X rays." In other words, "It can't be me!" We protect our egos by refusing to accept self-destruction. We are still "number one," and the obliteration of "number one" is unthinkable! Some responses are defiant, some are morose, and others even superciliant and devil-may-care. Still others will reject death by exhibiting a jovial and frivolous manner, using inappropriate clichés concerning death and unveiling reckless behavior or an attitude of invulnerability. This denial may become so intense that the physician's persistence in emphasizing a fatal prognosis is equivalent to repudiating the individual as a person, causing him to reject the physician-patient relationship.

2. *Reaction.* The second stage usually comes as the attitude of "It can't be me" changes to "Why me?" Becoming mad at God and mad at the world, he thinks, *How could God allow a thing like this to happen to me? What have I done to deserve this?*

3. *Recognition* is often the third stage. Many times there is a recognition that God exists. Although

78

patients may never have acknowledged the existence of God previously, at this stage they may bargain with God to help them. The attitude is "Save me, and I'll turn my whole life over to You." No longer able to deny his illness, the patient begins to recognize his situation and his dilemma. He tries to think of reasons why God should not allow him to die.

4. *Regression*. The fourth stage of death brings a sense of helpless remorse. The patient finally realizes there is no way to escape the process of dying. It is really happening to him! The resulting depression is a response to injury of the patient's self-esteem and self-image. The feeling of worthlessness preoccupies his thoughts, and he spends his time being nostalgic. While some patients are "protected" by a denial process that persists until the death event, others succumb to a chronic invalidism that may progressively increase until death occurs. Realizing there is no way out, the patient just gives up and loses his will to live. In contrast to the suicide threat, this decision to quit living can bring about death very quietly and effectively. We should be on the lookout to help patients through this depression stage.

5. *Resignation*. Resignation frequently occurs as the fifth stage. The dying person accepts his predicament and becomes resigned to his fate. Sometimes apathy or withdrawal may continue if depression persists and hope is lost. But for some, hope is not lost! Some people die with the perfect assurance that life-beyond-death for them will be better than life as we know it.

Many of these stages can be skipped or modified when the patient will openly communicate about his own future, his prognosis, and his disease. This communication can be between him and the doctor, the minister, the employer, friends, or members of his family: in short, *you.*

The family's attitude toward the dying patient tends to be more important than any other influence in the patient's life. Certainly the social agencies and social workers now assigned to care for the dying, though helpful, are really the least influential. Adapting to his illness, accepting the eventual possibility of death (not a mandatory concept), and gaining an awareness of a real life beyond death can possibly prove to be the salvation not only of the person's emotional stability but also of his soul and of his anticipated future. The family can aid or hinder the patient in this respect, depending on their own attitudes. Recognition of and resignation to his unwanted fate may become the family's challenge.

Mrs. Addie Ford is dying as I write these paragraphs. She's a dear friend whom I've had as a heart patient for many years. Her two daughters have been crying. Their mother has been told everything, and the daughters don't know how to discuss her death with her, much less the cancer that is causing it.

But I have noticed that everyone is sad except Mrs. Ford. She already knows what's wrong with her, and she keeps mentioning that she looks forward to seeing her husband again, who has been dead for several years.

Why shouldn't the daughters talk with her about the prospect of seeing her husband? What's wrong with discussing death with someone who is more than willing to talk about it? Death doesn't have to be horrible. To many elderly people it is beautiful—many actually have been looking forward to it as a sort of graduation or class reunion. They have their assurance of salvation through the Good News and would like to share the message with others. They've had time to contemplate and prepare, time not all of us will have.

For those who are already assured of a good afterlife, the fact that the moment of death is painless should provide additional comfort. Meanwhile, the doctor can keep the patient comfortable, and family and friends can share their love as the dying person journeys beyond death's door. Death does not of necessity have to be a sorrowful event.

STAGES OF BEREAVEMENT

Somewhat parallel to the emotional passages through which a dying patient proceeds, I have noticed discernible stages through which a grieving survivor passes as well.

Not all of us have had to face the death of a close loved one. In a 1977 issue of *McCall's* magazine, French actress Catherine Deneuve recalled the saddest event of her life—the death of her sister in a "horrible accident" ten years earlier: "We are not prepared for death. Instead of sex education in our schools, they should give a course in death education. In living you find out about sex—but dying, how do you find out about that?"

From my observations of bereaved survivors, I have noted a process of grief that usually contains three stages:

1. *Denial.* Much like the patient who realizes he is dying but denies it, the grieving survivor goes through a similar emotional reaction shortly after the death of a loved one. Intellectually, the survivor cannot accept the fact that the person is actually dead.

In denying death, survivors may act as if the deceased person is living in the home by keeping his or her room in order or by otherwise demonstrating that they have not accepted the loss of the loved one. Also, by denying the death, emotions such as sadness, anger, and crying go unexpressed. These pent-up feelings become overdue. Sometimes it may take as long as a year before one is able to admit, by open discussion, that his or her loved one is actually gone.

In my opinion, the denial stage is often prolonged because most priests, rabbis, ministers, and friends cease their visits to the bereaved after the first week or so following the funeral. To correct this, some counselors suggest that ministers or friends visit weekly for a while, then monthly. These visits not only help the survivor accept the fact that a death has occurred but also serve to help curb what will be almost inevitable: loneliness.

2. *Anger.* Once acceptance of the death event is accomplished, the grieving person often asks himself, "What did I do to deserve this?" At this point, anger and resentment set in.

There will be a great temptation for the grieving person to begin feeling sorry for himself. For the Christian, it is imperative to resist such temptations and to acknowledge the reign of Jesus Christ over all circumstances. Instead of selfishly wishing there had been "more time to spend" with the loved one who has died, one should begin to thank God for the abundance and joy of the years that were spent together.

3. *Reconstruction.* This is the stage of adaptation and reorganization that normally starts three or four months after the death of the loved one. It is here that a desire builds to get affairs in order and to make specific plans concerning the future.

Not all survivors undergo a difficult grieving process. It is easy for some and painful for others. Some may move out of the home they shared with their now deceased spouse, for instance, and drop all activities associated with their former life. In so doing, they eventually compound their loss. Others cling to the home and to objects identified with their loved one and thus refuse to face reality.

Whatever may be your own response when a loved one dies, it is crucial for you to know that your feelings are nothing new in human history; your grief will be somewhat predictable. Thus, the question becomes twofold: How can I deal with my own grief, and what can I do to help others live through theirs?

GRIEF COUNSELING

Grief counseling should not be left to psychologists, psychiatrists, funeral directors, or other people who are only transiently concerned with the spiritual and emotional needs of the bereaved. Everybody seems to want to refer the grief-stricken person to a doctor or psychiatrist for a sedative to suppress their emotions. This is the error of modern society.

The good, healthy bewailing cry of grief should be accepted as *normal* rather than treated as "sick." Trying to stifle the grief process can be destructive and seems to me to be typical of our death-denying society in America. Americans are more inhibited now in expressing love and grief than they were one hundred years ago. Fears and phobias about death have increased as religious convictions have decreased.

Strangely, the more affluent a person becomes, the more preoccupied he seems to become with his own death and the more he identifies with the death of others. Insecure in his own faith and future, he is afraid for himself and for others.

A prominent young ophthalmologist, and a new Christian, experienced the death of a close friend. The friend, previously in good health, fell dead on the tennis court while in the act of making a serve. No warning was evident. The ophthalmologist, also a tennis enthusiast, has since been hesitant to exercise in any manner without examining his blood pressure, his cholesterol levels, and also his stress electrocardiogram. He has subsequently changed to a radical diet and has a morbid preoccupation with his coronary status. He lives in fear of death. While professing a Christian faith, he is, in effect, denying his future and God's control over it. He is still maintaining the concept that death will be the end of it all. In addition, he has fallen into a trap shared by so many: He is apparently grieving for himself, not for his friend.

Most experts agree that it is very important that the

grief process be normally experienced and allowed to evolve. Grief groups can be and have been established where people share the loss of a loved one with others and describe what happened: how they existed after the loss, the types of successful occupational therapy they have found, and generally just how they have adapted.

At present, social workers and psychologists are about the only ones aiding families recovering from grief-stricken attitudes. Some people experience after-death depression that can lead to suicidal thoughts. Spiritual guidance is what is needed. Spiritually oriented auxillary professionals supported by trained volunteers should ideally be doing grief-counseling. Spiritual guidance should not be left to the secular-trained psychologists, social workers, doctors, or nurses who know nothing about it or couldn't care less. On the other hand, many ministers are unable to offer personal contact and counseling except on an intermittent and transient basis, which usually is inadequate to fulfill the need. Comforting the family after the loss of loved ones may be required for several weeks or months until adaptation to a new life occurs.

Do you want a ministry? Counsel the bereaved! Ask your minister to train groups of you first to minister to the dying patient and then to the bereaved family after death has left its mark. Comfort the dying. Comfort the bereaved. These are two neglected ministries. Unwanted, they've remained unfulfilled.

It is important to teach counselors of the bereaved or dying that it is *proper* and *expected* for people to cry and to express anger or bitterness when death occurs. We should not try to suppress their feelings or shut them up to "avoid the pain of reality." Grieving is a normal, natural process of releasing pent-up emotions. It is God's way of getting the feelings out where they won't be perpetually disturbing the person, slowing down his recovery.

Author Catherine Marshall received a letter from a man whose name was Sam. His wife, Helen, had collapsed and died from an unexpected heart attack at age forty-three, leaving him with three children. Sam wrote in part:

> If God is a loving Lord, why would he take Helen away from husband and children who need her so much?
>
> I am a church-goer, but this has shaken my faith; and I can't pray at all, and I know that when you've lost your faith, you've lost everything. If only I could find my way back to God instead of accusing and resenting Him, then maybe I could find the will to go on.[1]

Catherine Marshall answered Sam's questions about death and God's will:

> You ask where Helen is? Scripture tells us that Jesus Christ conquered this last enemy Death for us through His bodily resurrection. "Because I live, ye shall live also," is His ringing assurance. "If it were not so, I would have told you."
>
> Obviously, when we really believe in another life we are forced to rethink our limited viewpoint of death

[1]Catherine Marshall, "A Letter from a Grieving Husband," *Guideposts* (July 1979), pp. 10–13.

as the ultimate tragedy. You should ask yourself whether your grief is not so much for Helen as for your own loss.

So then, what about you and your loneliness? You wrote that you can no longer pray and that you are accusing and resenting God for Helen's death.

I think you should shut yourself in a room and tell God out loud exactly how you feel about Him in regard to Helen's death. To make connection with Him, ruthless honesty is necessary. I have done this in moments of despair and found, to my surprise, even a feeling of God's approval simply because I was being real.

But then you need to go beyond bitterness and anger. Why? Because grief is a real wound in the human spirit and that bitterness is effectively cutting you off from the only One who can heal that wound and give you answers and a reason to go on living.

God's promises to His children as recorded in the Bible are our legacy. But in order to obtain His inheritance, an heir has to step up and claim it. Here is one of the greatest of all promises for you to claim for yourself and your children: "And we know that all things (even Helen's death) work together for good to them that love God, to them who are called according to His purpose" (Romans 8:28).

. . . Finally, I want to give you a prescription to restore zest to your life. It is based on one of the immutable laws at work in our world: We get back what we give away.[2]

The mark of a successful grief counselor is his or her

[2]Ibid.

ability to listen. Counseling by listening is the essential ingredient to ventilation of the emotions. This is true in counseling the dying patient as well as the bereaved. Too many counselors want to do the talking and the advising. Nothing turns the recipient off faster. Wait until he asks for advice. It may take several visits.

The counselor must also be able to recognize those people who are not progressing satisfactorily so that they can be referred to mental health professionals. Reactions and unusual behavior common to neurosis or psychosis and hallucinations or delusions are usually signs of mental illness, especially if these symptoms become persistent or progressive.

Before making a diagnosis of mental illness, it is important to compare the personality of an individual prior to the death episode to his behavior during bereavement. Those who are terse, tight-lipped, and independent will remain so throughout the grief process. If someone tends to have an emotional personality, then hysterics and theatrical fireworks should be expected when bereavement occurs. Such behavior should be considered an exaggeration of normal personality, tendencies not necessarily symptoms of mental illness.

People need two things: emotional support and emotional freedom. You support them by just being there. Their freedom to rant and rave and to display their emotional response should be uninhibited. However, you should not respond to it or regenerate it. Just be there. Allow the person to freely express himself. This is good for the recovery process.

Not all people go through all the stages of grief. The spouse of someone dying with a prolonged illness has already experienced anger and remorse when he or she first learned of the disease. Emotional relief may replace emotional grief at the time of death, since the spouse believes that the loved one is finally free of suffering and pain.

Others, of course, will persist in denial and anger for many months if they will not accept the fact that the loved one has died. This is when they particularly need the reassurance that life after death does occur, as these resuscitated patients persistently tell us and as the apostle Paul reminds us: "We are confident, I say, and well-pleased rather to be absent from the body and to be present with the Lord."[3]

Psychologist John Fox of Pasadena, California, mentions that the greatest hindrance in counseling people, besides a real love for that person, is a lack of communication. When it is a young person being counseled, it is usually not a "generation gap" problem that hinders us but a "communication gap." Dr. Fox gives us some aids in counseling:

1. *Listening.* Many of us have preconceived ideas and do not listen. We are instead too anxious to impart our own knowledge and ideas.
2. *Understanding.* We must "accept" the person and truly comprehend why he feels the way he does. We must not deny his feelings.
3. *Communicating.* The person must comprehend and feel that we are one with him. Insisting that we should stop acting with selfish motives, Dr. Fox quotes the Bible: "Let nothing be done through

[3] 2 Corinthians 5:8.

selfish ambition or conceit, but in lowliness of mind let each esteem another better than himself. Let each of you look out not only for his own interests, but also for the interests of others. Let this mind be in you which was also in Christ Jesus . . . ."[4]

He also mentions that we should never "talk down" to the client, informing him why we think he should feel this way or that. Instead, we should approach the person with sympathy, love, and understanding. The real purpose of counseling is to support the patient with suggestions and possible solutions and to offer spiritual support as much as physical assistance.[5]

In summary, the acceptance of death is easiest for families who have a firm belief in life after death and especially if the loved one has a personal relationship with Jesus Christ. The Christian faith offers a consistent solution and is one of the main reasons I am personally interested in supplementing the numerous secular courses now available on death and dying with those that contain spiritual guidance and support. Such Christian guidance is vital to our mental and emotional welfare when it becomes our own turn to be the victims of some lethal condition.

[4]Philippians 2:3–5.
[5]The above information was taken from a personal letter to me from Dr. John R. Fox.

PART II

Preparation For Dying:
Who's Right?

CHAPTER VI

The Search Begins:
Understanding Death

Even though I have been a medical doctor for years, until recently I effectively ignored serious thought on the topic of death, something I had seen almost daily. Then through the experiences of my resuscitated patients—out-of-the-body experiences in an afterlife—I became more interested in what really occurs at death. Not only was my interest professional, but it became profoundly personal. Was I ready to face what might await me after death? Would I win the bet? I didn't know.

So I began research on death, and the results of many observations of patients and studies resulted in my first book, which I've already mentioned. The book immediately aroused a controversy because several readers seemed surprised that something other than bliss might await some people when they die. The media had a field day, and more often than not, quotations were not accurate. One article in particular outdid the others.

Never in my life had I been so misquoted. The article included the experiences of patients reported on in my book. Its conclusion was one of universal forgiveness.

BEFORE DEATH COMES

After we die, we enter a timeless dream world where happy people roam breathtaking mountains and valleys. Nobody works. There is no pain, no sickness, no evil. Money and material goods do not exist.

That's the picture of life after death put together by researchers who have studied the experiences documented by people who died, then were resuscitated.[1]

Well, that certainly isn't what half of my patients reported! After-death experiences are not all good. This is an important point, because if everybody had a "good time" in the next life, then we could all "eat, drink, and be merry." The reincarnation concept would be encouraged. The gates of heaven would be open wide, and salvation would be universal—an undeniable right.

Such is far from the truth of these reports. The patients who have actually tasted death briefly tell us that the afterlife does not appear to revert back to this world at any time, as the reincarnationists would have us believe; nor is this next life always a good one, as the humanists would maintain. In fact, the fear of judgment is the one thing that seems to concern these patients most—and this judgment is what they see and experience while they exist in spirit form. They do not enter into another physical life or into someone else's body. My research indicates that there is a separate existence in the spirit world, and after this life we are *not* reincarnated. There seems to be a heaven or a hell awaiting us in the next life.

[1]"Life After Death—A Dream World of Beauty and Happiness." *National Enquirer* (June 12, 1979), p. 41.

REINCARNATION AND HUMANISM

Let me ephasize again how the reports of resuscitated patients *differ* from the claims of reincarnationists. My patients say:

1. The next life occurs in an entirely different world than the present one. After separation from the body, the spirit is transported, frequently through some tubular conveyance, to another world that is completely different from the one left behind. There is no indication of ever returning to this world.

2. The circumstances in the next world do not resemble the present world, historically or otherwise.

3. The people they meet in the next life always represent loved ones or acquaintances who have died in *this* life—not in "other lives."

4. The next life is apparently unending. There is no indication of re-entry into lives in the present world.

5. The afterlife is either good or bad without any "in-between" existence.

Of the vast amount of religious literature reviewed, the Christian Bible most closely describes the experiences of these patients. And the Bible doesn't teach reincarnation.

The most important part of preparing for death is knowing what will happen to you after you die. Contrary to the wishes of many, there is no indication that you will be reincarnated here on this earth; rather you will continue to live in a new world, either in heaven or hell. At least, that's what many resuscitated patients say; and the Bible confirms their conviction.

But how about *déjà vu* and "past-lives" recall? Are these satanic? How can I tell who is right? To seek answers to these questions I embarked on an amazing journey, and perhaps you will find it surprising also. I had to find my way, before death gave me an unchangeable verdict. The search was filled with many pitfalls, for it's easy to be deceived—even about things that should be clearly understandable. I know from experience.

IT'S EASY TO BE DECEIVED

One hazy summer day I was piloting my plane and approaching DeKalb County-Peachtree Airport outside of Atlanta. I called the tower and received clearance to land on runway 27. As I approached the runway I noticed there was no other traffic at all. This seemed most unusual. When I was about a hundred feet off the ground, I noticed several fighter-jets arranged in precise order along the runway. I said aloud to myself, "I've got the wrong airport! This must be Dobbins Air Force Base several miles west of DeKalb-Peachtree!" I shoved both throttles forward on the Aztec and got out of there fast. If I had landed, there would have been a fine to pay.

What had happened, I reasoned later, was that this airport also had a runway 27. I was landing on the right runway at the wrong airport, talking to the wrong tower! What a mistake! I have been kidded about it ever since. Things don't always appear to be what they seem to be. This is equally true in regard to the death riddle.

Many people solicit answers from palm readers, interpreters of tarot cards, Ouija boards, divining devices, and horoscopes. Untold amounts of money are spent. It seems that man always wants to see into the future in an attempt to control his own destiny—anything to escape the grim reaper. In ancient Rome the Caesars consulted the soothsayers before making decisions involving risk. Even before that period of history the problems fostered by man's insecurity gave birth to astrology. To escape loss or death is the name of the game. The search for happiness is secondary.

Subsequent religions seemed to be born out of man's search for a relationship with God and an understanding of life and death. My own interest in life after death led me to study these religions. After a laborious study of comparative theology in the sacred books of many religions, including the Torah and Talmud of Judaism; the Koran; the Vedas, Upanishads, Brahmanas of Hinduism; the Avesta of Zoroastrianism; the sayings of Confucius; the Agamas of Jainism; the Tripitake of Buddhism; the Kojiki of Shintoism; the Tao-te-ching of Taoism; and the Analects, I have discovered that the one book that is the most descriptive of the after-death experiences of resuscitated patients is the Christian Bible! Yes, that dusty old book lying on your shelf and mine.

This finding served as a stimulus for me to gather further opinions and beliefs from the man on the street. My travels to discuss my previous book served admirably in presenting to me a wide spectrum of people for study.

THE MAN ON THE STREET

As I traveled about the country, I had the opportunity to talk to taxicab drivers, persons in studio audiences, talk-show hosts, cameramen, hotel bellhops, people in restaurants—persons from most walks of life. The subject of life after death always seemed to engender a response. Everybody had an opinion.

One taxicab driver, for instance, while we were enroute to a radio station, stated: "I thoroughly agree . . . there is life after death . . . I've always believed in reincarnation."

When I asked the taxi driver if he was of the Christian faith, he said, "Yes, I've been going to church all of my life." His belief in reincarnation puzzled me, because I could recall no mention of it in the Bible.

When I arrived at this radio station in New York City, I noticed that two other guests were going to be on the same program. One was a fellow physician, a psychiatrist, and the other was an author who had written almost fifty books, many of them dealing with subjects in parapsychology.

When the host asked this prolific author if he believed in the Bible, he replied:

> I believe in most of the Bible but not in Genesis. That book certainly was completely written in error. There is no question that Buddhism explains much better these multiple lives that we lead. Reincarnation has been experienced by many people throughout history. The life in which they return is always commensurate with the deeds they performed in the previous body. The Buddhist wheel of life is forever turning as each of us is continually reincarnated from death back into another earthly life.

THE SEARCH BEGINS: UNDERSTANDING DEATH

The psychiatrist, an orthodox Jew, stated that he practiced mysticism and believed in the occult sciences. He said:

> I have actually hypnotized one of the clairvoyants of national repute who has been assisting the New York police in an uncanny fashion. Under hypnosis she obtains clues, clues so accurate that they invariably lead to the solution of unsolved mysteries.

The author who had written so many books on the occult later indicated that he was an avid student of Edgar Cayce—the "sleeping prophet"—who popularized reincarnation in the United States. This was something else I had to add to my "search."

The investigation was enlarging. Unanswered questions were accumulating. I began spending more time in the libraries of each city I visited.

My next stop in New York was for an interview with a lady who is a professional promoter of people and books. She was to promote my book and arrange a closely packed itinerary in several large cities.

As we digressed now and then in our discussion of the book promotion, this young woman said that life after death was a good subject that should interest most people since it involves everybody. As time went on, the conversation got deeper. She said that she personally believed in a heaven and hell. She told me:

> Because of this I try to help people. Not many people know it, but I used to be an alcoholic. Some of those I help are not only on alcohol but some are on drugs. Some are homos and some are something else. Everybody's got something. We even have a mixed

group who are addicts on different things, and they meet in my apartment every Friday for group therapy under a psychiatrist who is a personal friend of mine. He is a wonderful man. He has helped most every one in our group, and this makes each of us want to help others. So, if there is a heaven, I don't have to worry. I'm a good girl, so I know I'll get there!

I made a mental note that this philosophy didn't sound just right. What if more was required to get to heaven than just "being good?" I knew the Christian Bible claimed that faith in Christ was required for entrance to heaven. What did the books of other religions have to say?

This incident recalled to mind a conversation I once had with a Jewish lady whom I met while giving a talk in Tel Aviv, Israel. She was an interesting person. She had completely divorced herself from her own religion. She said that she had always endured the hardships of being labeled a Jew, but she still had no desire to follow the Jewish faith.

Here she was in Israel on tour with her husband, a physician, but she had no desire to see Jerusalem or any of its great heritage. Instead she had gone to Tel Aviv to see the collection of fine art. While her husband was at the Wailing Wall, she was in Tel Aviv. She pictured her husband as a devout Jew and herself as an outcast, one denying her birthright and wanting nothing to do with it. This apostasy does not seem uncommon, and I wondered why.

Suppose, similarly, I had been born into a Jewish, Moslem, or Buddhist family instead of into my own. My concepts of life and death would perhaps be entirely different. Certainly they would not be Christian! Does each religion worship the same God by a different name? How did all the religions get started? Are they related? If so, why would Christ say, "I am the way, the truth, and the life. No one comes to the Father except through Me"[2]? And why then do the Scriptures state, ". . . there is no other name [besides Jesus'] under heaven . . . by which we must be saved"?[3]

As I mentioned, if I am betting my life on what I believe, then I can't afford to be wrong. If life after death is eternal, then I'd really better find out what this is all about. Although no one had ever explained the world religions to me, I knew each one claimed to have an answer to the same age-old question of what happens to you when you die. It was so pivotal I knew I would have to search the religious literature myself. This was too important to trust to the opinions of others. I wanted to know firsthand since my whole future was at stake.

The search had begun. Many major religions hold as a basic belief that God is the source of life. Is He? Is there a God? This question had to be answered before I could look at what the proponents of religion and philosophy had to say.

<hr>

[2]John 14:6.
[3]Acts 4:12

CHAPTER VII

Understanding Life

To begin my search I wanted to find out if there is a God or if there is really nothing "out there." My research had indicated that those who had died and had been resuscitated came back quite firm in their belief in God. But how could *I* be sure? Perhaps I could find a clue by looking not at death, but at life. Since death starts with life, perhaps we might examine one to learn about the other.

First of all, how did we get here? Did we arise from a reincarnation "continuum," living one life after another and having existed forever in the past? Or were we "handmade" and placed here on earth for a one-time purpose? Or did we spontaneously evolve from the lower animals who in turn arose from cellular life, mothered from the mud of the primordial "ooze"? Thus, to talk about death or the ending of life, we need to consider birth or the beginning of life.

There are two contrasting worlds of thought here: evolution versus creation, or otherwise stated, humanism versus theism. *Humanism* is a philosophy based upon the belief that man shapes his own destiny. Humanism maintains that man is as much a natural phenomenon as an animal or plant; man was not supernaturally created but is the product of evolution; he is not under the control or guidance of any supernatural being but has to rely on himself and his own powers. This is the philosophy posed by the late Sir Julian Huxley, a British biologist.[1] It is also propounded by George Galord Simpson, professor of paleontology at Harvard University, who says that man ". . . owes to no one but himself, and it is to himself that he is responsible. He is not a creature of uncontrollable and undeterminable forces, but his own master. He can and must decide and manage his own destiny."[2]

In contrast to this is *theism* which states that God created everything that exists. Although my twenty years of formal education were primarily based upon concepts of evolution, I since have learned through medical observations that simple creatures cannot become more complex by the process of mutation. Because almost all mutations are destructive, I have concluded that it really takes more blind faith to accept evolution than it does to accept creation!

Dr. Lane Lester, professor of biology at Liberty College in Lynchburg, Virginia, after reviewing scientific and moral issues involved in modern test-tube babies, cloning, and genetic engineering, states:

> Most scientists are evolutionary humanists. They believe that man is an evolved animal and responsible only to himself. On that basis, humans have no more dignity than a fruit fly and no more right to life.

[1] Sir Julian Huxley, *The Observer* (July 17, 1960), p. 17.
[2] George Galord Simpson, *Life of the Past* (New Haven, Conn.: Yale University Press, 1953).

BEFORE DEATH COMES

Humans have dignity because they have been created in God's image. Unless the people who receive the benefit of genetic engineering also receive God's cure for their sick spirits, it will be like putting cosmetics on a cancer.[3]

Evolutionists or humanists will themselves admit that 99.9 percent of mutations are harmful or neutral in their effects, and they will also admit that simple creatures cannot become more complex by mutation. Nevertheless, because of their great *faith,* they believe that the entire history of life has been produced from mutations.

Dr. Thomas Barnes, professor of physics at the University of Texas in El Paso, mentions a disagreement he had one day with another scientist while they were traveling in an airplane. Dr. Barnes pointed out that evolution is always governed by the laws of science. The other scientist agreed. He also agreed that the most basic law of science is the First Law of Thermodynamics, which states that matter and energy can neither be created nor destroyed. This means that matter has been in existence forever. Dr. Barnes continued, "Now you're in trouble, because the Second Law of Thermodynamics says in effect that even though energy has been here all along, it is becoming less and less available for use."[4]

Apparently Dr. Barnes's traveling companion had no good reply. Dr. Barnes had merely pointed out the degradation process. You and I are not getting younger,

[3]*Creation Dialogue,* vol. 6, no. 2 (Mar.–April 1979), p. 3.
[4]Edward F. Blick, "Evolution: Science vs. the Bible," *The Gospel Truth* (Oct. 1979), p. 6.

for instance, we are getting older. Water runs downhill, not uphill. This degradation law is basic in science and its effects are unending. Thus the whole universe is running down from some original point of existence. Dr. Barnes states that he doesn't have a problem with this fact: "I postulate a great God who created the world and wound it up and now it is running down, just as all the laws of physics say it should."[5]

It is obvious that the universe had to come into being, but the laws of science do not provide for such an occurrence. Science must postulate the initial conditions that lie outside of the laws of science. Where did the original matter come from to create the universe? If one claims the universe has been here forever, then he must discard the Second Law of Thermodynamics, because the universe would have totally run down a long time ago. We would not be here.

Dr. Barnes is saying that true science imposes constraints that make evolution impossible and that it is time to expose evolution as the "nonscience" it is.[6] To me evolution, like creation, is a belief, thereby a faith.

TO FIND THE END, SEARCH THE BEGINNING

To find my own answers in regard to evolution, I began to read Darwin's *Origin of the Species*. While formulating his theory of evolution, Darwin was on a trip around the world in an old sailing ship and spent much of his time in the Galapagos Islands. This small group of isolated and rather barren islands lies six

---

[5]Thomas G. Barnes, "The Scientific Issue," presented to the Professional Educator's Workshop, Nov. 22, 1975, Lubbock, Tex.
[6]Ibid.

hundred miles westward off the Pacific coast of Ecuador.

To duplicate and relive what Darwin saw, I felt that I, too, must go to these islands. My trip took me first to Peru and then back to Ecuador where I boarded a military aircraft of the Ecuadorian government, which then took me to the islands. We landed on an abandoned World War II airstrip. Since we were near the equator, the day was hot and sunny. After riding a dilapidated tour bus with failing brakes, we arrived about two miles down the road at a dock berthing a small private cruiser that was to take us on a tour of the islands. We had been furnished a guide, a zoologist with a Ph.D. degree. With a thick German accent she explained the characteristics of the various animal species as we encountered them. The captain of the cruiser, taking the craft close to several of the barren, rock-like islands, allowed us to see at close range the peculiar animals that were natural inhabitants of these areas. Besides the seals and peculiar fish, one that particularly interested me was the blue-footed booby, a bird larger than a sea gull with a very long beak and peculiar blue feet that are webbed like a duck's.

I remembered the defects in the theory of evolution that baffled Darwin the most. They were the transition of amphibians to mammals, with the marsupial and platypus as examples of inadequate bridging between species. Neither were there examples to illustrate a transition between crawling and flying creatures, or between apes and man. The fossil strata were also a source of dilemma, for they have never been in "proper" order.

The platypus, for example, is a funny looking crea-

106

ture with deep brown, velvety-feeling fur similar to the seal's, but it has a flat bill like a duck's and no teeth once it reaches maturity. Its feet, although webbed, are ideally designed for scratching and digging. It lays eggs, but when the young hatch they nurse. But instead of sucking nipples, the baby platypus licks its mother's under-surface, causing milk to flow from the hair-ends of the fur. The male platypus has a hollow spur on the inside of its heel that is supplied with venom as potent as that of a poisonous snake. Its legs are short and parallel to the ground, much like the legs of a lizard. It has cheek pouches like a monkey.

Untrained in comparative zoology, I asked the zoologist which biological group the platypus belonged to: fowl, reptile, or mammal? She was uncertain. Perhaps it could be considered a transition from almost anything, but the simplest explanation of its existence, I would think, is simply that God made it the way it is!

It seemed evident that the rugged species found on these islands have endured without any reported change for untold numbers of years. Nor has there ever been a new transitional form evident on these islands since Darwin's visit.

MUTATIONS

Precise orderliness is in everything, everywhere. A watermelon seed never produces any other fruit. Watermelon seed always leads to a watermelon! Seed-to-fruit to seed-to-fruit, there is no chaos in reproduction. The only time chaos appears is when a mutation occurs, allowing a cancerous fruit to develop—which, much like cancer growths in humans, destroys its own self and also results in the death of the host harboring this reproductive chaos. In either event, the mutation doesn't result in the production of peaches or apples! It only results in a grotesque, deformed, and short-lived watermelon. The malignant change is always recognizable for what it is.

Mutations are usually self-destructive, rare, and never have been shown to result in a completely different species. But the theory of evolution is based upon mutations as the origin of new species with survival of the fittest! In fact, however, "good" mutations are usually so bad that we actually consider all mutations bad.

Any deviation in precise orderliness—whether defects in genes, chromosomes, or amino acid configurations in the DNA (deoxyribonucleic acid)—are usually lethal, or grotesque enough that we wish they were. And the possibilities of deviation are tremendous. Just to display the possible variations of the genetic code in the DNA molecules making up the chromosomes of one mammalian cell would require about one million pages of 8½ by 11 inch paper.[7] Only God could produce uniformity in this complexity. The chances of spontaneous appearance would be about as great as having a computer evolve from a junk pile blasted by a stick of dynamite.

Mutations have never been shown to result in even a new organism, much less in any new specie within a specie. In any event, they could not account for the 1.7 million different forms of protozoa, plants, and animals that exist in the world today. Because mutations are rare and could occur only in perhaps one in a hundred thousand events, we see that the change required to

7"Genetic Revolution," *M. D. Magazine* (Aug. 1979), p. 77.

evolve a reptile into a bird would not only require a fantastic number of mutations, but all of them would have to be beneficial to the animal. As I mentioned, mutations are often harmful.

To disbelieve that there is a Creator takes a stupendous faith compared to the little bit of faith required to believe that there is a God, a Creator of all life. Thus, there is apparently not one chance in billions that life on our planet occurred as an "accident." If it couldn't have been an accident, then how did it happen? Who created life?

Howard B. Holroyd writes:

> Physical scientists, who know higher mathematics and who are capable of analytical thinking, should never have allowed the thoroughly mistaken mechanical theory of evolution to reach such a degree of apparent certainty in the thoughts of nearly everyone."[8]

Further admonition of the evolutionist is given in the foreword by Dr. W. R. Thompson to the new edition of Darwin's *Origin of the Species.*

> As we know, there is a great divergence of opinion among biologists, not only about the causes of evolution but even the actual process. This divergence exists because the evidence is unsatisfactory and does not permit any certain conclusion. It is, therefore, right and proper to draw the attention of the non-scientific public to the disagreements about evolution. . . . This situation, where men rally to the

[8]Howard B. Holroyd, "Darwinism Is Physical and Mathematical Nonsense," *Creation Research Society Quarterly*, vol. 9, no. 1 (June 1972), p. 13.

defense of the doctrine they are unable to defend scientifically, much less demonstrate with scientific rigor, attempting to maintain its credit with the public by a suppression of criticism and the elimination of difficulties, is abnormal and undesirable in science.[9]

GEOLOGIC FINDINGS

Geologic findings also indicate a sudden, not evolutionary, origin of life. In the lower (older) strata of geologic rock, the evolutionist would expect to find fossils of simple life forms, and in the higher levels fossils of more complex creatures. The findings are to the contrary. In both levels the geologic fossils found are complex. The lower Cambrian layer, containing most of the major groups or organisms, makes it evident that these life forms must have appeared suddenly and not gradually. This finding was baffling to Darwin himself. He found that not one of these fossils showed a transitional intermediary between one species and another. There were several "missing links." They weren't found then, and they haven't been found since.

Darwin recognized this problem himself when he wrote:

Long before the reader has arrived at this part of my work, a crowd of difficulties will have occurred to him. Some of them are so serious that this day I can hardly reflect on them without being in some degree staggered . . . why if species have descended from other species by fine graduations, do not we

[9]Charles Darwin, *Origin of the Species* (New York: Hill & Wang, Inc., 1979), Foreword.

everywhere see innumerable transitional forms? . . .
why then is not every geological formation and every
stratum full of such intermediate links? Geology as-
suredly does not reveal any such finely-graduated
organic chain and this, perhaps, is the most obvious
and serious objection which can be urged against the
theory. . . .[10]

ETERNITY AND THE THEORY OF RELATIVITY

Are there any clues furnished by science that would
indicate the existence of the apparent eternity my patients describe in life-after-death experiences? Surprisingly, perhaps, the brilliant findings of Albert Einstein
relate to this question.

Last year, 1979, was the year of "Einstein," marking
one hundred years since Albert Einstein's birth in Ulm,
Germany. Like most geniuses, Einstein was bored with
school. He was only interested in mathematics and
physics, and when the family later moved to Italy, Einstein continued his studies in neighboring Switzer-
land, receiving his Ph.D. degree in 1905 in Zurich.
With a superior, highly complicated intellect, Einstein
began at the age of sixteen to write papers and propose
scientific theories beyond the most advanced knowledge of his day. When only twenty-five years of age, he
presented four theories that basically changed scientific
thinking and produced the atomic space age. These
were the theories of relativity, mass energy equiva-
lents, Brownian motion, and the photon theory of light.
The Einstein equation—"$E = MC^2$"—made possible the
splitting of the atom and the production of the first

[10]Ibid. (New York: J. M. Dent & Sons, 1956), p. 80, 157.

agents of nuclear destruction. The relativity theory opened the universe to man. Einstein's concept of the relation of time, space, and matter presented the speed of light as one possible way to explain and enter the pathways to eternity itself! The Scriptures mention another entranceway: death itself. Einstein's theory only suggests what Scriptures have always claimed: that eternity does exist.

What did Einstein himself think of the concept of a Creator and a Sustainer of the universe? He said:

> God is subtle, but He is not malicious. I cannot believe that God plays dice with the universe. Strenuous intellectual effort and contemplation of God's creation are the angels which will lead me, reconciling, strengthening and yet with uncompromising rigor, through all disquiets and conflicts of this life.[11]

Einstein's contemporary, another great scientist, Dr. Werhner von Braun, said:

> We may be very certain that our starward strivings fit somewhere into God's plan. Humanity has never learned that lesson of refraining from great deeds when the Master of creation has put into their hands the means of accomplishing them.[12]

There remains that great mystery of earth's creation: Of all places in the universe, why did God so love this insignificant and tiny earth that He gave it life and then revealed Himself through His Son? "For God so loved the world that He gave His only begotten Son, that whoever believes in Him should not perish but have

[11]*Science News* (Mar. 31, 1979), p. 213.
[12]Helen Walters, *Wernher von Braun, Rocket Engineer* (New York, N.Y.: Macmillan, 1964), p. 123.

everlasting life."[13] So far, we haven't found life elsewhere. Why did God so love our world and not some place else? I can't find that answer. If I could, the key to understanding life and death would probably be close by.

STOKING THE SOLAR FURNACES

Did God create the universe? If so, making us as creatures would have been an easy task by comparison. And if He could make a universe, then He could just as easily have made a heaven and a hell, I would think.

Astronomers (not to be confused with astrologers) have mapped some of the universe and have shown the earth to be a tiny speck in space, one of nine major planets orbiting a star, our sun, which is itself so big that one million earths could fit into it. Yet our sun is only a little star, whose life-sustaining fires are derived from a nuclear furnace that is already middle-aged and getting older. Our sun is relatively insignificant, being only one of two hundred and fifty billion stars swirling in a great spiral of stars we call the Milky Way.

Many of these other suns (or stars) may have planets of their own. Yet we are told by Frederic Golden, science editor of *Time* magazine, that our Milky Way is just one of the millions upon millions of similar galaxies or collections of stars. The Milky Way is said to be so far separated from our neighboring galaxy of Andromeda that it takes light more than two million years to reach us, even though light travels at 186,000 miles per second or some six trillion miles in a year.[14]

---

[13]John 3:16.
[14]Frederic Golden, *Quasars, Pulsars and Black Holes* (New York: Pocketbooks, 1977), p. 15.

Indeed, our universe is so vast and far-flung that its immense size is beyond human comprehension. Our fastest existing rockets could not carry us to the nearest star beyond the sun in less than many hundreds of years. At the speed of light, the nearest star, Proxima Centauri, is 4.3 light-years away. An expedition across our own galaxy would take us a hundred thousand light-years, or millions of years by ordinary spacecraft speed.

The universe is not tranquil or static but is constantly moving, occasionally interrupted by events of awesome violence. Stars explode with unimaginable fury, and whole galaxies are ripped apart. Swirling magnetic fields, many times stronger than the earth's, whip particles through space at greater speeds than those achieved by our most powerful accelerators.

Our earth itself is really a spaceship, and you and I are astronauts, whether we like it or not. While our earth is traveling at 18 miles per second, our own solar system is moving onward at 150 miles per second.

It is only in the past few decades that astronomers have begun to understand how stars evolve and continue burning for untold numbers of years before they extinguish. When Albert Einstein published his theory of relativity in 1905, the continual firing of the thermonuclear furnaces of stars was first explained. By the deceptively simple equation, $E = MC^2$, part of the solution of the mystery was evident. E stands for energy, M for mass, and C for the speed of light in a vacuum. However, the speed of light, multiplied by itself, is such a large figure that even a tiny amount of mass is equivalent to an enormous amount of energy.

In fact the sun (as first suggested in the early 1920s by

British physicist Arthur Eddington) is largely a great burning ball of very hot hydrogen. Burning hydrogen in thermonuclear form is also the main ingredient of all the billions of other stars like the sun. Thus, the thermonuclear furnaces of all the suns of the whole universe have been stoked and fired by the Creator through God's secret formula for stars, the formula of hydrogen atoms.

A whole chain of reactions occurs in this thermonuclear furnace. As hydrogen is converted into deuterons and helium, there is a weight loss in the whole reaction of less than one percent. This seemingly small loss of mass yields a fantastic amount of energy. It is because this loss of mass and size is so slight that the sun can keep burning for countless eons without noticeable reduction in either heat output or size. Our God is pretty smart!

Furthermore, unlike the *fission* reactions in conventional nuclear power plants on earth, *fusion* reactions of the stars do not produce any great amounts of radioactivity. If God's secret were revealed to us and the sun's thermonuclear fires could be duplicated on earth, then mankind would have a virtually inexhaustible energy source without attendant fears of dangerous radioactivity. Do you think God will eventually allow us this discovery? Or will the energy crisis be our downfall?

WHO'S BEHIND IT ALL?

If we are to understand the meaning of death and life after death from patients' reports, it is essential to know first if God really exists, as we previously discussed, and also if He is the Creator holding dominion over life and death.

It seems to me that man has an inborn knowledge that he is related to God and made in His image. This relationship always seems to surface when calamity strikes. Felled by acute injuries and brought to the emergency room, for instance, the patient sooner or later will be heard to call out, "God help me" or "Jesus save me." When the chips are down we seem to revert without thinking to communion with our Creator. It occurs automatically! The saying is true, "There are no atheists in foxholes." We could also say, "There are no atheists in hospital emergency rooms." Some day even those now denying God will find themselves calling on Him.

Having a view of God formed through philosophical speculation is entirely different from viewing God as a living Being who controls the universe and to whom we shall be held accountable.

The existence and power of God can never be "proved" by the scientific method any more than history can be "rerun" in the laboratory. The scientific method is useful only in dealing with measurable things. Although God cannot be proved, the fact remains that the vast majority of human beings and the cultures of all ages have always believed in the existence of God or gods.

The universe itself, a remarkably complex and precise cosmos of physical order and infinite complexity, also speaks of a Creator. How could a cosmos of order possibly evolve from a chaos of confusion? The very heavens declare the glory of God. This is evident to everyone who looks.

Albert Einstein, admittedly one of the greatest scientific minds of all times, said:

> My religion consists of a humble admiration of the illimitable superior Spirit who reveals Himself in the slight details we are able to perceive with our frail and feeble minds. That deeply emotional conviction of the presence of a superior reasoning power, which is revealed in the incomprehensible universe, forms my idea of God.[15]

Whenever we look at the inside of a watch, a computer, a radio or a television set, we become confounded with the circuitry and intricacies of design. Instantly we know that it was created by nothing other than an intelligent mind. And the universe and its physical laws are much more complex and intricate than any gadget!

CAN GOD BE FOUND?

"Canst thou by searching find out God? . . ."[16] The answer, of course, would be no—unless God revealed Himself.

Fortunately, we have already been "the visited planet," as J. B. Phillips aptly puts it, visited by God in the form of man and manifested in the birth, life, death, and resurrection of Jesus Christ. Although it is impossible for the finite to penetrate the infinite (that is, for us to find God), it is possible for the infinite to penetrate the finite (for God to find us). This is, of course, exactly what God has done as simply expressed in Hebrews 1:1,2: "God, who at various times and in different ways spoke in times past to the fathers by the

[15]Lincoln Barnett, *The Universe and Dr. Einstein* (New York: Morrow, 1957), p. 95.
[16]Job 11:7.

prophets, has in these last days spoken to us by His Son. . . ."

You still want "proof" of God? The very heavens you've admired have always proclaimed the existence of God. This is stated clearly in Psalm 19:1–4.

> The heavens declare the glory of God; the skies proclaim the work of his hands. Day after day they pour forth speech; night after night they display knowledge. There is no speech or language where their voice is not heard. Their voice goes out into all the earth, their words to the ends of the world. In the heavens he has pitched a tent for the sun.

The apostle Paul also indicated that man has always known about God through inborn knowledge and instincts and that unbelievers will have no excuse when after death they face judgment before God.

> For the truth about God is known to them instinctively; God has put this knowledge in their hearts. Since earliest times men have seen the earth and the sky and all God made, and have known of His existence of great eternal power. So they have no excuse. . . .[17]

[17]Romans 1:19,20; *The Living Bible* (Wheaton, Ill.: Tyndale House, 1971).

CHAPTER VIII

The Fourth Dimension: Heaven and Hell

Investigations into the origins of life and the mysteries of the universe have led me to conclude that the facts are consistent with the existence of a Supreme Being—God. But what did the facts have to say about my next life? Is there a heaven and a hell? Or is there nothing?

Not all religions agree that death is the entry to an eternity of either heaven or hell. If there is a hell, however, then I'd better know so I can avoid it. It may not be safe to die.

It may seem surprising, but as I have already described, patients who have returned from clinical death fear post-death judgment but not death itself. Death, these patients report, is surprisingly painless—no more than the sensation of a missed heartbeat! All of us seem to have an innate fear of death, but fear of judgment is *not* something we think about much in our day.

We should remember that the notion of accountability to God is nothing new or novel. The truth is that predictions of heaven and hell pervade all of history and most religions. Yet very few people seem concerned about the possibility of judgment after death.

"How could a loving God send anybody to a place like hell?" they say.

There are at least fifty passages in the Bible that use the word *hell* and twice that many other passages that refer to a place of eternal damnation. Furthermore, nearly every writer in the Bible spoke of hell. Even Jesus had a great deal to say about it.

Many people deny the existence of a place of eternal torment. Nevertheless, *hell* continues to be one of the most popular words in conversation. A lot of people apparently don't believe in the very place where they continually tell others to go.

WHAT ABOUT HEAVEN?

Patients always love to tell about their good afterlife experiences. They are eager to recount these wonderful events. However, among the numerous reports it's easy to detect those people who are fabricating a story. Without knowing it, those who are recounting reliable experiences always report a sequence of events that parallels what others have reported. An individual may miss one or two events in the sequence, but the other events are always consecutive and recognizable. The normal sequence is very similar to the following case:

> I could see the other car swerving before he jumped the median. Out of the corner of my eye I could see that he was coming right at me. There was no way I could get out of his way. I said, "This is it." Although I was never sure I believed in God, I remember saying, "God help me!" Then the last thing I remembered was hearing this terrible crash with glass splintering like an explosion. The steering wheel must have gone into my chest, it hurt so much.

THE FOURTH DIMENSION: HEAVEN AND HELL

In a split second the explosion was gone and then the pain was gone; I knew I must be dead! I remember other cars stopping and people peering into the car through the broken windows; it all seemed so strange.

It was then that I knew I had been looking down on the scene of the accident, completely free of pain and without a worry in the world. I felt completely at ease, just floating up there. I heard one of them say, "Call an ambulance." They were dragging my body out of what was left of the car. The driver of the other car already seemed to be dead.

After they had stretched me out on the ground, one of them started blowing through my mouth and another one pushing on my chest; it was hard for me to believe that that body was actually mine!

Traffic seemed to be piled up for a half mile behind the accident, and I could hear an ambulance trying to get through.

By this time I heard a strange noise and then found myself tumbling head over heels through some big tube or tunnel. It was awfully dark in there, but I was glad to see a light at the far end which seemed to get bigger and bigger. I got out into a beautiful valley lit by something as bright as the sun, but I couldn't tell where it was coming from.

And there I saw both of my parents (who had died before) coming to greet me down a pathway between these large groups of trees and flowers. They seemed awfully glad to see me and said they had been looking for me. Each put an arm around my waist, and we walked down the path deeper into the valley where we came to a stream. It was too wide to cross without wading. As I was getting ready to cross this stream, I felt something like a baseball bat suddenly hit me in the chest and everything went black.

I awakened to find myself back in my body at the scene of the accident. Everything was hurting. They were applying an electric shock from a "defibrillator" gadget. Afterwards, I felt sad about leaving my parents and that place in the valley. It was so beautiful. I can't describe it.

Instead, I was back here, all bloody and cut up and on my way to the hospital.

Now, this wasn't a dream. I've had many dreams, but this was something completely different. I know I was there, and I won't be afraid to go there again.

Did this patient have a glimpse of heaven? To answer my own questions I began to study the various beliefs of people throughout the world. I began a search for the faith that most closely resembled and explained the experiences that these patients had had in the world beyond death.

At first the questions seemed entirely unanswerable. But then, as different situations arose, I would find a little bit of an answer here and there, some in this city and some in that. I would visit the libraries, searching the literature and reading the sages of the past. I began to record and summarize the teachings of many faiths. In a word, after traveling around the world and talking to people of different faiths and reading the holy books of many religions, I have come back to the Judeo-Christian Scriptures, which best reveal what these patients tell me. The Bible promises everlasting life to those who are willing to place their lives in safekeeping with Christ.

WHAT ABOUT HELL?

In contrast to heaven, the subject of hell is never popular. Resuscitated patients don't like to mention it, and no one else likes to talk about it either.

Whatever happened to hell anyway? You don't hear about it much anymore—unless, of course, someone tells you to go there! In my own church I asked my minister why he didn't preach more about hell. He frankly told me, "Because the congregation wouldn't like it."

A Gallup Poll back in February, 1978, found that only thirty-nine percent of Americans believe that there is a hell. Moreover, only one in eight of these believe that this hell could pertain to them.[1] In a poll of divinity students taken way back in 1961, fifty-six percent rejected the virgin birth of Jesus Christ; seventy-one percent rejected that there was life after death; fifty-four percent rejected the bodily resurrection of Jesus Christ; ninety-eight percent rejected the concept of a personal return of Jesus Christ to earth.[2] Many practicing ministers go even further and reject altogether the belief in a personal God.[3]

No doubt, hell is not a popular subject. Although hell

[1]George H. Gallup, *The Gallup Poll* (Wilmington, Del.: Scholarly Resources, Inc., 1978).

[2]Jhan and June Robbins, "The Surprising Beliefs of Our Future Ministers," *Redbook* (Aug. 1961) p. 108.

[3]Ardis Whitman, "The View From the Pulpit," *McCall's* (Feb. 1968), p. 147.

(or its equivalent) is mentioned 167 times in the Bible, I find that almost forty percent of the ministers I encounter are not at all sure there even is a hell, or ever was one!

This change has apparently occurred in the last one hundred years, since earlier preachers warned of "hell's fire" as one of their basic conversion motivation tools. Recently, three ministers in my home town (and some in other cities) have privately taken me aside after one of my talks and said, "Come now, Dr. Rawlings, you don't really believe there is a hell, do you? These patients couldn't be right when they say they've been there. They're dreaming! Everyone knows that hell just doesn't exist!"

Yet, Jesus repeatedly said hell is very much in existence. Reviewing my Bible, I notice that Jesus talked more about matters of hell and judgment than He did about heaven. He must have thought the subject of hell was of great importance!

If most nations, states, cities, courts, families, and individuals still believe in punishment for wrongdoing, why should God's right to punish be denied? Why disbelieve God's Word that hell is a real place made for punishment of the wicked? Instead, hell has become a "figure of speech," and seldom do people think of it as an actual place of eternal torment.

Our generation has developed a strong conviction that beliefs held in the past are outdated and probably incorrect. Jon Braun commented about how "moderns" view hell.

> . . . hell is a concept invented by the ancients that fits nicely into the ignorant life-schemes of antiquity and

124

medieval times. Now with the advent of our marvelous age of "enlightenment," such creations of the past can be shunted to the scrap heap reserved for dilapidated and antiquated ideas and can be replaced by modern, relevant, enlightened, and existential truth. . . .[4]

The centers of learning throughout North America abound with professors now offering scientific evidences for an assortment of hypotheses that life after death is nonexistent or that hell does not exist. Others say there is a "continuum" for everyone, and that there is a transition at death from one life into another; each person is born anew as another person or thing. While authentic scientific evidences for these hypotheses are, of course, totally lacking, there are testimonies by those who have recalled past lives in minute detail after *déjà vu* experiences. Such experiences may be prompted by evil powers; they are not from God.

Some believe that hell is an experience of your own doing, the way you presently choose to lead your own life. Others say, "How could God send anybody to a place like hell? That would make Him worse than Hitler!" Still others say, "Since the Bible says God is Love, how could a loving God invent a place like hell?" Or you hear the thought of hell dismissed like this: "There is good in all of us, and if there is a heaven, we'll get there."

Because the subjects of life after death, heaven, and hell are hotly debated with everyone having an opinion, I receive many bizarre letters. Here are a few examples:

[4]Jon Braun, *Whatever Happened to Hell?* (Nashville: Thomas Nelson, 1979), p. 15.

. . . both religion and hell are merely the results and outgrowths of sick minds preoccupied with sex and masturbation.

Doctor, you should have a leave of absence and take a trip down the sawdust trail. . . .

Hell is found in your present life if you choose to live that way. It doesn't exist in the next life because there is no "next life."

In my travels I find similar reactions among my fellow physicians. Doctors have approached me in the hallways of hospitals inquiring about my interest in life-after-death research. Some will chide me and say, "How's God today, Brother Rawlings?" Others will poke a little fun and ask, "Where are you preaching this weekend?" These comments, I have noticed, are usually meant for the benefit of an audience. They are not made in private.

Other doctors might say, "Keep up the good work, Rawlings; I am a Christian, too." But I notice the doctors who are Christians usually mention it when no one else is around, when no other doctors, nurses, or even patients might overhear the Christian identification. For some reason, there still seems to be a reluctance among physicians to identify themselves with spiritual matters.

These doctors, as well as some of my patients, seem to be afraid that other people will find out they are Christians! This is true as well among lawyers, engineers, educators, and other professional people. They act as if they were a member of the Ku Klux Klan or some other secret organization!

I had always been that way myself—embarrassed to

be identified as a Christian. I thought it detracted from my status or indicated weakness or an inability to take care of myself.

This attitude among doctors concerning spiritual concepts seems to be uniform throughout much of the world. During medical lectures in Peru, Israel, and Australia when I have asked for a vote from doctors if they thought there was a heaven or a hell, the response was two to one against life after death in any form. It is only recently that physicians have developed an inquiring interest and have indicated that they should not relegate investigation of the afterlife to psychiatrists or others who do not resuscitate and observe patients in the emergency-room setting.

If you were to limit your study to volunteer patients who have had a life-after-death experience, you would think there is a heavenly adventure awaiting everyone who dies. That this is not so was the amazing result of studies made immediately after resuscitation events, before patients could dismiss or conceal their "bad" experiences. Now we are finding just as many hell experiences as heavenly ones among these revived patients![5]

Do you think these patients who claim to have seen hell are right? All of these experiences seem to be similar in terms of the sequence of events after one leaves the body. How could each person dream the same sequence? For instance, it would be most unusual if you and I reported having had the same dream last night. But if a whole room full of us had had the same dream,

[5]Maurice Rawlings, *Beyond Death's Door* (Nashville: Thomas Nelson, 1978), p. 25.

that would be impossible! Yet this is what is happening—patients are telling us the same "dream," which to them is not a dream at all, but reality.

There were a number of afterlife scenes recounted in my earlier book, about half of which were from very disturbing, negative experiences from the other side. Many other such reports have accumulated since that time. For example, this one occurred just recently.

> I had just sat down from cheering as the Vols came on the field to meet the Yellow Jackets before a real exciting game. Here on their own home field, Tennessee should have an edge over Georgia Tech. I guess the excitement got to me. I felt my heart skipping a little bit just as it had six years ago when I had my heart attack. I had felt very well ever since my bypass surgery, but here it was again, this vague discomfort in my chest. Right in the middle.

> The next thing I knew everything was turning black, and I must have fainted because that's all I remember for the next three days. I was unconscious until I started hearing my wife's voice whispering in my ear. I remembered no pain after the blackout occurred, but I do remember some very strange happenings. Frightening ones!

> I found myself suddenly out of my body and into another existence. I had gone through a deep tunnel into a pit. At least it seemed to be a pit, but I'm not sure what it was. I'm not sure where it was, either. But it certainly wasn't in this world. It was somewhere else where there was a roaring noise and objects coming before me like pieces in a puzzle. I knew that I had the job of fitting those pieces together. I knew I must do it quickly to keep something worse

from happening. It was horrible! Things just wouldn't fit and they moved so fast I'd only have a second to try and fit one piece to another before they would be gone and another one would appear in its place. They were sort of suspended in space, different colored objects with peculiar ends on them. Most of them would be oblong and one end wouldn't match the other. I started crying out loud, and then I started screaming—but nobody would pay any attention. I could hear other voices all around me, but I couldn't see anyone. There weren't any flames or fire, but I knew this was hell. It was so terrible I just can't tell you about it. I can't find the words that would describe what I saw. It just wouldn't stop.

I'll never know how I got out of there, but the next thing I remember was my wife's voice in my ear. She was saying, "Give it all to Jesus! Give it all to Jesus!" And I finally did. Right then I called on Him to save me and take over my life. People may not believe me, but this is the truth. I have had dreams and nightmares, but this was different. This was hell. I'm convinced of it. I saw it. If only other people could see it!

In a hospital bed this patient related this story to me in a husky, quiet voice and with tears in his eyes. He had been successfully defibrillated by a portable electrical unit used by the emergency medical technicians who manned the ambulance at the football stadium. They had started manual resuscitation in the stadium and continued it in the ambulance until he had arrived at the hospital. After he had stabilized, he was transferred to our hospital in Chattanooga.

Hell as another "kingdom" is repeatedly mentioned in the Bible. And as I noted earlier, while we expect to be punished by civil law for wrongdoing in the present life, why do we choose to believe that God will not punish us for wrongdoing in the next life? Would it seem more unjust at that time than it does now? He has, after all, given us ample warning about what will happen if we reject God's plan of salvation from punishment. Whether you or I think it is "fair" has nothing to do with it.

The Scriptures speak so clearly to this issue:

> And do not fear those who kill the body but cannot kill the soul. But rather fear Him who is able to destroy both soul and body in hell.[6]

Job described hell as,

> . . . the land of gloom and deep shadow, to the land of deepest night, of deep shadow and disorder, where even the light is like darkness.[7]

Even though Jesus spoke more about hell than He did about heaven, some people who believe in Jesus Christ say there is no hell. Listen to what Jesus said about it.

> "When the Son of Man comes in His glory, and all the angels with Him, then He will sit on the throne of His glory. And all the nations will be gathered before Him, and He will separate them one from another, as a shepherd divides his sheep from the goats. And He

[6]Matthew 10:28.
[7]Job 10:21,22.

130

will set the sheep on His right, but the goats on the left. . . . Then He will also say to those on the left hand, Depart from Me, you cursed, into the everlasting fire prepared for the devil and his angels: . . . And these will go away into everlasting punishment, but the righteous into eternal life."[8]

The Bible tells me that Christ cannot lie. Since He said hell exists, I must take Him at His word.

Do you think hell will really last forever? Christ answered that question this way.

"And if your eye makes you sin, pluck it out. It is better for you to enter the kingdom of God with one eye, than having two eyes, to be cast into hell fire— where 'their worm does not die and the fire is not quenched.' "[9]

What will happen to men who turn their backs on God and follow beliefs based on their own reason?

"The Son of Man will send out His angels, and they will gather out of His kingdom all things that offend, and those who practice lawlessness, and will cast them into the furnace of fire. There will be wailing and gnashing of teeth."[10]

And the sea gave up the dead who were in it, and Death and Hades delivered up the dead who were in them. And they were judged, each one according to his works. And Death and Hades were cast into the lake of fire. This is the second death. And anyone not

[8]Matthew 25:31–33,41,46.
[9]Mark 9:47,48.
[10]Matthew 13:41,42.

found written in the Book of Life was cast into the lake of fire.[11]

But just "being religious" doesn't mean much. In his book, Jon Braun has a word we all should heed. *"Instead of inventing complaints of how cruel and unjust hell is, we should come to faith, and glory in how creative and gracious God's provision of deliverance from hell is!"*[12]

This certainly seems to be true. God has a wonderful future planned for those who accept His "passport to heaven." For example, ponder what Job had to say.

> "I know that my Redeemer lives, and that in the end he will stand upon the earth. And after my skin has been destroyed, yet in my flesh I will see God."[13]

And in the New Testament, Paul told the Corinthians in his first letter to them:

> Behold, I tell you a mystery: We shall not all sleep, but we shall all be changed—in a moment, in the twinkling of an eye, at the last trumpet. . . . For this corruptible must put on incorruption, and this mortal must put on immortality. . . . then shall be brought to pass the saying that is written: *"Death is swallowed up in victory. O death, where is your sting? O Hades, where is your victory?"* The sting of death is sin, and the strength of sin is the law. But thanks be to God, who gives us the victory through our Lord Jesus Christ.[14]

[11]Revelation 20:13–15.
[12]Jon Braun, *Whatever Happened to Hell?* (Nashville: Thomas Nelson, 1979), p. 176.
[13]Job 19:25,26.
[14]1 Corinthians 15:51–57.

Finally, Jesus made a promise too. Among the very last words Jesus spoke is this reminder.

"Behold, I am coming quickly, and My reward is with Me, to give to each one according to his work."[15]

Yes, there really is a heaven and a hell. It is not just my patients who tell me this. God says so, too!

THE SECOND TIME AROUND

Perhaps because of uneasiness prompted by the Word of God, it appears that contemporary man has called up an old "cop-out" as a means of circumventing man's accountability to God: *reincarnation*. The myth is almost as old as the human race itself. And frankly, if one chooses to sweep aside what God tells us about our future, I suppose having hope for some sort of reincarnation is as good a substitute as any. If I were personally going to trust my own hunches as opposed to God's revelation, I would certainly choose reincarnation over, say, annihilation!

A Chicago taxi driver was telling me all about reincarnation on our trip to a television station where I was to be interviewed. Amazing! He must have assumed that *everyone* believed in reincarnation, just as I had at one time assumed that everyone was a Christian.

When I arrived at station WBBM in Chicago for the interview, one of the hosts of the show asked me, "What sign were you born under, Dr. Rawlings? I usually ask this question of the guests on the show so I'll

[15]Revelation 22:12.

have an idea of how well they will perform that day. This usually helps them to know whether they should come on strong or whether they should tone it down."

This was the first time I was made aware of the great importance some people attach to horoscopes for guidance in daily living. I made a mental note that I must learn more.

The next morning at KSTP-TV in Minneapolis-St. Paul, I was escorted into the "green room" to wait for my appearance on a ten-minute segment of the hour-long "Morning Show." I found myself talking to two ladies and a man who were also waiting. They were to present a segment on hair styling. The man would demonstrate the most recent coiffures available, using the ladies as examples. One of the women, who had a rather elaborate hairdo, became very interested when she learned my subject was "life after death." She told me that she was a Taurus and was investigating the probability that she was living a second life. By consulting a mystic, she was "retrogressing" through previous experiences to identify who she had been the first time around.

"How did you first become interested in reincarnation?" I asked.

She replied, "Well, I started reading my daily horoscope in the newspaper and comparing notes with my girl friend. It was really interesting. From astrological surveys of our birth dates, we found the right thing for us to do each day. I didn't know about reincarnation until my girl friend said she had been investigating her past lives. She was convinced that she had recognized places as if she had been there before."

I made another mental note—*astrology and rein-*

carnation—both antedating Christianity by several thousand years—are still common in the thoughts of many, many people.

THE REAL CULPRIT

During rounds at the hospital recently, one of the nurses inquired about a patient who had just died in the intensive care unit. She said, "Do you really think this fellow went to heaven? My minister tells me that we all do if we go to church, but that doesn't explain *déjà vu*, which I've always heard is true—that we enter into life again when we die, becoming some newborn babe in another body but always remaining ourselves inside."

This intermixture of ideas I find is a very common thing even among Christians, and their ministers are frequently unaware of these notions among members in their congregations.

Translated, *déjà vu* means "already seen," and it is used to substantiate another version of reincarnation dating back to the origin of the Hindu religion.

Unknowingly, the nurse was mixing two completely opposed ideas to form a new faith. She was thus, probably unintentionally, molding her own image of God. As it says in Romans 1:23, man "changed the glory of the incorruptible God into an image made like corruptible man. . . ."

But my contention was in the minority on another occasion when I spoke in sunny California. I found thoughts similar to those of the nurse among the group of students (many of them from UCLA) who populated this spiritist church that day. They were very devout, attentive, and reverent. You could have heard a pin drop! They seemed to enjoy the service and appeared to believe what they heard. They liked the idea of God viewed in an image that was pleasing to man. Furthermore, they had felt they had been very fair by incorporating the "best of all religions" into their faith.

This new religion didn't consider man as made in God's image, but God made in man's image. In their view, God is in man; therefore, man is himself God! And concerning life after death, who wants to contemplate the possibility of heaven or hell? Why not be assured that you are coming back to this world and that the existence of "hell" is only imaginary?

This ideology is very palatable. If there is no sin, there is no hell! No salvation is necessary! This attractive religion is particularly appealing to collegians, who account for some 30,000 converts a month. I call this new religion "Babylon" and will discuss it more later.

CHAPTER IX

Death, Reincarnation, and the Occult

"Your students say that you have studied many religions and have been teaching in the Temple of Self Realization for many years. Do you think religions have anything in common?"

"Yes," the Swami replied to my question, "if you look you will find that all religions are interrelated and all of them worship the very same God only by using different names; but it's still the same God. That's why our Universal Religion of the new age should be recognized by all. We are brothers under the skin, looking for the promise of life after death. This brings all religions together. They are all interested in eternal existence after physical death."

"Why did you choose Hinduism as the basic foundation of your Universal Religion?" I asked.

"Because Hinduism is concerned with the eternal being of your true self—your soul—rather than emphasizing the soul's relationship to God. The soul is detached and not an agent of sin. There is no sin and there is no hell. Hell is the way you live in your own life. It only exists here on earth.

"Thus we can consider the central creed of Hinduism as the concept that the universal spirit reincarnated from one life to another, without beginning or end, is the highest manifestation of God found within man—within yourself. You are yourself God! You must come to this through Self Realization."

"What must I study to learn more?" I asked him.

"Read the Vedanta."

And so I did. I read the Vedanta, including the Upanishads and Bhagavad-Gita and many other Hindu commentaries. One of them, *The Vedanta for Modern Man,* had as its central theme that Brahman, or God, is in existence everywhere and indwells everything.

> What we adore in a Christ, a Buddha or a Kali or Jehovah or Kwan-yin is our own eternal nature. This, therefore, implies that the . . . Vedanta must do homage to all divine personalities since all our expressions are of the one truth of Brahman. . . . We may claim with some assurance that the Vedanta philosophy is superior to Christian theology as a potential bridge between science and religion . . . . the world-picture presented by Vedanta is largely in accord with the latest theories of astronomy and atomic physics. . . . The Vedanta also teaches the practice of mysticism . . . through meditation and spiritual discipline, without the aid of any church or delegated ministry.[1]

It was interesting to find that the Congress of World Religions, when summoned in London in the 1930s, quoted Ramakrishna's ecumenical statement of a new universal movement in world religions, which ends with the thought—"all roads lead to God."

[1]Christopher Isherwood, *The Vedanta for Modern Man* (New York: New American Library, 1951), pp. 10–13.

This concept of the all-encompassing divine spirit is found in many of the sacred Hindu scriptures. From the ancient passages of the Bhagavad-Gita, I quote from Krishna, the assumed seventh reincarnation of the god Vishnu:

> Whatever path men travel
> It is my path.
> No matter where they walk,
> It leads to me.

Since there is no hell in the Vedanta, you can't lose. Krishna saves everyone. You will live again. Everyone gets in!

Going back to the library for help, I found this statement by American adherents of Hinduism.

> The Vedanta . . . urges us to look beyond the differences [in religions] in order to realize the unity of all faiths, for the highest manifestation of God is found within man—that eternal and unswavering Self which is beyond dogma or doctrine. In man himself lies the supreme unity, and it is there he must begin—and end—his search. This is the message of Vedanta.[2]

In essence, then, the basic concept of far-eastern religions is the "supreme unity." Man does not need help outside himself. Capable of healing himself, improving himself, saving himself, he is God.

The Swami's Universal Religion, its basic concepts evolving from a selection of beliefs from all religions, has

[2]Clive Johnson, *Vedanta* (New York: Harper & Row, 1971), p. 6.

reincarnation as its base. Since reincarnation is obtained from the Hindu faith, I wondered how that religion got started.

Raga Rammohan Roy, a man of wide learning in Sanskrit, Greek, and Hebrew, in 1830 became the political founder of modern India and the father of a new religious movement. Raga Roy reformed Hinduism and grafted in some of the ethical teachings of the Gospels, particularly the Sermon on the Mount, but rejected the miraculous and theological claims of the New Testament. He emphasized a universal religion based on morality and rationality. Not only was he one of the pioneers of early universalism, but he could also be considered one of the first pioneers in women's liberation. His social reforms in India included the abolition of "sati," the custom of burning alive the widows of deceased husbands.

Further liberalization of Hinduism occurred in 1875 when Swami Sarawati established Hindu universalism that declared the faith open to all people of all castes, removed image worship, and ended child marriage and pilgrimages. Some old practices were preserved, such as observing the sanctity of the cow.

Political independence in India followed the era of religious reforms under Mahatma Gandhi. Gandhi died in 1948 after teaching that total self-control, which was accomplished through meditation and good works, was basic to the search for truth.

As we mentioned, Hinduism today has a fundamental concern with reincarnation, the time-cycle process of rebirth into another state commensurate with a person's good or evil actions in the preceding life.

I attended a church service that presented still another

aspect of the New World Religion (my label for these universalist religions). In the sermon I noticed that the guru started with the Gospel of John, then progressed to the Vedanta and the Koran, and finally combined all of the thoughts into a beautiful philosophical message that showed we should love one another.

I posed a few questions to the guru after the message. "What happens to you when you die?" I asked.

"When a man dies," he said, "his soul comes out of his body and immediately enters into the body of a newborn babe. If the man leads a bad life, he might be born as a cripple or in poor health or perhaps as a laborer."

"Suppose this man continues to lead one bad life after another?" I asked.

"Then," he said, "he keeps being born again into worse sickness and sufferings as a result of his own karma."

I thought to myself, *Perhaps my trash man is really a bad person from a previous life—I better not have anything to do with him or with cripples or the lame or the blind; they are probably being punished!* This is indeed, I was told, the thought of many Hindus who purposefully neglect the plight of others.

RELIGION TODAY

The increasing focus in America today on Hinduism and reincarnation, astrology and the occult, psychic phenomena and parapsychology, may mark the revival of many ancient pagan religions. No longer must we select only from variations of Christianity, Judaism, or Islam; now a whole gamut of man-made religions are available and acceptable.

However, it was these man-made religions and the various religions of the occult that were specifically condemned by God in the Old Testament and which continue to be condemned today. They include astrology (including horoscopes), witchcraft, sorcery, magic, spiritism, and psychic phenomena. As in the past, these religions continue to rely upon powers of the occult. Obtaining secret knowledge from evil spirits, the practice of sorcery as we know it today was also practiced among the ancient nations surrounding Israel. It was for this very reason that God took land away from the Canaanites and gave it instead to the Jews for their Promised Land.

Israel was prohibited by God from allowing sorcerers, spiritists, mediums, or other agents of the occult to be in their midst.[3] These occult practices and the Christian faith are, for the same reason, completely incompatible.

Nevertheless, an occult religion is predicted to become dominant in end times. The growing emphasis on the occult is illustrated by the following examples.

On a TV program entitled *Psychic Phenomena, the World Beyond,* a young British girl appeared with music inspired by the spiritualist world. She was sponsored by a journalist who was interested in spiritualism and married to a British medium. The response to her TV appearances was overwhelming, and the demand of the viewers for live concerts became intense. As a result, this girl commented, "The gods are opening many doors for me so that the light can be shown. It is wonderful to share with others the gifts from the spirit world." She

[3]Exodus 22:18, Leviticus 19:26, Deuteronomy 18:10–14.

attributes her success to her psychic guides in another world.

Some of the many letters I have received since my first book was printed are emphatic in their opposition to Christianity. They say that God is not in charge of our destiny, that we ourselves decide what we are going to be after we die. For instance, consider the following letter:

> . . . but as long as men [sic] are told there is a god, a benevolent power to take him to heaven or throw him in hell, man can never be in charge of his own destiny. So I would like to say that I am convinced that we should choose by thought, word and deed what experiences we are going to have after we die. *We and we alone* decide our *destiny*. May the knowledge of *true knowing* be man's guide.

Still another letter:

> If you only knew the true spirit realm of the dead ones, you would know the comfort indicated for one's future. There is no hell. How much respect would you have for a god who would put a person in a place of eternal torment? I have prayed God would reveal my dead 19-year-old son's spirit to me somehow and now I am beginning to see him in my visions when I meditate.

Although people's beliefs are fascinatingly varied, I notice that each person considers himself the final authority.

Tracts are sent with some of the letters to serve as

proof. These pamphlets describe Pyramid Power, the Church of Astrology, the Church of Religious Science, Astara, and so on. There are worshipers in various secret sects of the occult. Examples would be the cult of the All-seeing Eye and the Illuminati cult.

Seminars on the supernatural are now increasing in popularity. The following are some of the topics offered at one seminar: combining realms and interrelated knowledge of the metaphysical; holistic educators; astrologers; mystic healers; integral yoga; Kabbala (presented by a Rabbi); etheric surgery; psychedelic experience; guides to interspace; and study of biofeedback. This international conference included fifty participating workshops for parent-child sharing, allowing children an opportunity to express themselves. The family subjects included science fiction, psychic films, parapsychology, holistic health, psychic phenomena, and psychotronics. None of the subjects of orthodox religious faiths or their sects were listed. Of the sects, only one was invited to give a presentation: the Sufi offshoot of the Islamic faith.

What does God think of these various teachings today? God revealed His views to the apostle John who was allowed to peer into the future where he saw a woman riding upon a scarlet beast. The woman had this title written on her forehead:

MYSTERY
BABYLON THE GREAT
THE MOTHER OF HARLOTS
AND OF THE ABOMINATIONS OF THE EARTH[4]

John continued, "And I saw the woman, drunk with

[4]Revelation 17:5.

the blood of the saints and with the blood of the martyrs of Jesus."[5]

And then John wrote that he saw another angel coming down declaring:

> ". . . Babylon the great is fallen, is fallen, and has become a habitation of demons, a prison for every foul spirit, and a cage for every unclean and hated bird. For all the nations have drunk of the wine of the wrath of her fornication, the kings of the earth have committed fornication with her, and the merchants of the earth have become rich through the abundance of her luxury."

> "Therefore her plagues will come in one day—death, mourning, and famine. And she will be utterly burned with fire, for strong is the Lord God who judges her."[6]

Babylon may well represent those religious practices and places condemned by God. What will happen to Babylon? God says, "She will be utterly burned with fire." And they shall see the "smoke of her burning." God will display His anger. God is displeased, describing Himself as a "jealous God":

> "You shall have no other gods before me. You shall not make for yourself an idol in the form of anything in heaven above or on the earth beneath or in the waters below. You shall not bow down to them or worship them; For I, the LORD your God, am a jealous God. . . ."[7]

[5]Revelation 17:6.
[6]Revelation 18:2,3,8.
[7]Exodus 20:3–5.

145

If God did not spare His own people, the Jews, from punishment for their disobedience and their worship of other gods, how then will He spare any who are now worshiping nebulous "great spirits" concocted from the "best of all religions" and who are paying only lip service to Christ?

God warns us to avoid concepts resembling humanism; we do not control our own destiny, and we are not responsible only to ourselves. Speaking to the Israelites, God said:

> You may say to yourself, "My power and the strength of my hands have produced this wealth for me." But remember the LORD your God, for it is he who gives you the ability to produce wealth, and so confirms his covenant, which he swore to your forefathers, as it is today. If you ever forget the LORD your God and follow other gods and worship and bow down to them, I testify against you today that you will surely be destroyed. Like the nations the LORD destroyed before you, so you will be destroyed for not obeying the LORD your God.[8]

God also warned of the dangers of our present practices of the occult: " ' "Do not turn to mediums or seek out spiritists, for you will be defiled by them. . . ." ' "[9]

As God warned the Israelites entering the evil nation of Canaan, so He warns us today about entering evil areas.

> Let no one be found among you who sacrifices his son or daughter in the fire, who practices divination

[8]Deuteronomy 8:17–19.
[9]Leviticus 19:31.

146

or sorcery, interprets omens, engages in witchcraft, or casts spells, or who is a medium or spiritist or who consults the dead. Anyone who does these things is detestable to the LORD, and because of these detestable practices the LORD your God will drive out those nations before you. You must be blameless before the LORD your God.[10]

A bit later in this same chapter in the Bible, we read how God wants us to avoid psychics and parapsychology. He tells us also how we are to determine who are the true prophets of God.

But a prophet who presumes to speak in my name anything I have not commanded him to say, or a prophet who speaks in the name of other gods, *must be put to death* [italics mine]. You may say to yourselves, "How can we know when a message has not been spoken by the LORD?" "If what a prophet proclaims in the name of the LORD does not take place or come true, that is a message the LORD has not spoken. The prophet has spoken presumptuously. Do not be afraid of him."[11]

What should we do with such false prophets? God says in Leviticus 20:6, " ' "I will set my face against the person who turns to mediums and spiritists to prostitute himself by following them, and I will cut him off from his people." ' " He further insists: " ' "A man or woman who is a medium or spiritist among you *must be put to death*. You are to stone them; their blood will be on their own heads" ' " (italics added).[12]

[10]Deuteronomy 18:10–14.
[11]Deuteronomy 18:20–22.
[12]Leviticus 20:27.

And so it is today with enchanters, astrologers, mystics, and psychics—they are not to be compared with God's prophets of the Old Testament.

In the modern revival of the ancient occult arts, there seems to be the same ancient power of evil behind it all, perhaps more deceptively clothed today in an appealing "humanism," the "new reality of all faiths," or in the "one world religion." As predicted, this germinating religion is unifying and silently usurping the traditional world religions, replacing them with the new Babylon. Although such "religious" ideas are appealing to man, they are an "abomination" to God.

This brings me to the main point. I have a disturbing message for you. In my travels I believe I have seen something that the ministers and clergy do not see. Since they usually don't visit churches outside of their own faiths, they haven't witnessed this new camouflaged cancer that is attracting the young and the old alike.

I am saying that I have seen the amalgamating new world religion in embryonic form. Beware of her! Babylon is not yet to come; *Babylon is here!*

CHAPTER X

Preparing to Die: Who's Right?

How does one prepare to die? With all of the assorted spokesmen and gurus for countless religions and philosophies bending your ear, how can you find the truth and be confident that your decision is the correct one?

After many months of comparative reading and study, I found at least *two distinct ways in which the Bible differs from all of the other sacred books of the world!* It contains numerous accounts of both miracles and prophecies. Many researchers throughout history have found the same thing, I'm sure. But I found it for myself, and I felt very good about this because I'm not a Bible scholar. I have to do research the hard way. But if I can do it, so can you!

Although miracles have been recorded in many ancient religions—by astrologers, pharaohs of Egypt, Hindus, Muslems, and soothsayers—nevertheless, none of them were as spectacular, accurate, consistent, and unfailing as those recorded in the Old and New Testaments of the Bible.

However, the most impressive difference between the Christian Bible and all other holy books is the presence of *prophecy*. Other than the forecasts of life after death and what would happen to you if you weren't a good person, none of the other religious literature contains prophecy. In my studies I came to an astounding realization that if the predictions of the Bible's prophets could be proven unerringly correct, this should substantiate that the God of the Bible and the God of the universe are one and the same! I could then risk my very soul on the knowledge that Jesus Christ is truly the Son of God, and that in Him and Him alone, God became man. I would no longer need to be concerned with other books and other religions. I would know who I am, why I am here, and where I am going.

I first examined what the Bible says about history and science. As my investigation began, I noticed that the Bible was composed of sixty-six books that seemed to be incorporated into a complementary whole. It was written by some forty separate authors over a period of fifteen hundred years and has been preserved intact down through the centuries without any apparent alteration or magnification. This itself is a miracle to me!

I noticed that the Bible seemed to have an effect on individual men in history, upon individual nations, and particularly upon the course of history itself. Its historical accuracy, as substantiated by subsequent archeological confirmations, seemed far superior to that of the written histories of Assyria, Egypt, Persia, India, China, or other nations that I could study.

The Bible not only predicted future events but also many scientific facts that man would not discover until some time later. The Bible described the roundness of the earth (Isaiah 40:22), the hydrologic cycle (Ecclesiastes 1:7), the vast number of stars (Jeremiah 33:22), the increasing law of entropy (Psalm 102:25–27), the importance of blood in life processes (Leviticus 17:11), the atmospheric circulation (Ecclesiastes 1:6), among others.

PAST PROPHECIES

There are two types of Bible prophecy: the fulfilled and the unfulfilled. The fulfilled prophecies have been one hundred percent accurate, as far as I can verify them. Doesn't it follow, therefore, that those yet unfulfilled will also just as accurately come to pass?

More than three hundred Old Testament prophecies pertained to the first coming of Jesus Christ and were made hundreds of years before the events occurred. Things of the smallest detail were included in the predictions. For example, ancient prophecy foretold that Jesus would be an heir to the throne of David (Isaiah 9:7); He would be born in Bethlehem (Micah 5:2); the exact year that the Messiah would be born (Daniel 9:25); He would be born to a virgin (Isaiah 7:14); His ministry would be primarily in Galilee (Isaiah 9:1,2); He would be rejected by the Jews (Isaiah 53:3); His triumphal entry into Jerusalem would be upon a donkey (Zechariah 9:9); He would be betrayed by a friend (Psalm 41:9); He would be sold for exactly thirty pieces of silver (Zechariah 11:12); He would be silent when accused by false witnesses (Isaiah 53:7); He would be smitten and spat upon (Isaiah 50:6); He would be crucified with His hands and feet pierced and would bear our sins (Isaiah 53:4,5); He would be given gall and vinegar (Psalm 69:21); His body would be pierced (Zechariah 12:10); soldiers would cast lots for His coat (Psalm 22:18); He would be buried with the wealthy (Isaiah 53:9); He would not be allowed to undergo corruption and death, but He would be resurrected (Psalm 16:10); and He would ascend on high (Psalm 68:18).

There were also dozens of prophecies concerning the future of cities, nations, kingdoms, and dynasties. Some of them included the fall of Babylon (Isaiah 13:19, 20 Jeremiah 51:36–58); the total destruction of Nineveh (Zephaniah 2:13–15); Egypt's decline and her conquest by Babylon, Persia, and Rome (Ezekiel 29, 30, and 31); and the destruction of the city of Tyre by Nebuchadnezzar (Ezekiel 26:1–11). There are many others.

The most remarkable fulfillment of prophecy concerns the nation of the Jews—Israel. This is critical because the Jews serve as God's timepiece and seem to be related to every event that has occurred and will occur in biblical prophecy.

As an example, Daniel had accurately predicted that Christ would come as Israel's promised Savior exactly *483 years before* the event occurred (Daniel 9:25). Daniel also predicted that a Persian emperor would conquer Babylon, free the Jews, and then give the Jewish people authority to rebuild Jerusalem. Jerusalem was in ruins at the time of this forecast. Daniel went a step further and boldly named the Persian emperor who would allow this to be done. He said his name would be Cyrus. And so it was! Cyrus the Great conquered Babylon in 536 B.C.

The prophet Isaiah separately foretold the same event a hundred and fifty years before it occurred, stating that Cyrus of Persia would take Babylon by a surprise attack. In the ancient scrolls (on view today in the umbrella-like modern library outside of Jerusalem) one can see the old book of Isaiah on display. Isaiah 44:26–28 and 45:1, read:

PREPARING TO DIE: WHO'S RIGHT?

". . . Who says of Jerusalem, 'It shall be inhabited,' of the towns of Judah, 'They shall be built,' and of their ruins, 'I will restore them,' who says to the watery deep, 'Be dry, and I will dry up your streams,' who says of Cyrus, 'He is my shepherd and will accomplish all that I please'; he will say of Jerusalem, "Let it be rebuilt," and of the temple, "Let its foundations be laid." This is what the LORD says to his anointed, to Cyrus, whose right hand I take hold of to subdue nations before him and to strip kings of their armor, to open doors before him so that gates will not be shut."

In accordance with Isaiah's prophecy, Cyrus besieged Babylon in 539 B.C. Two gates to the city had been carelessly left open. Through the gates the Persian scouts infiltrated the city and diverted the Euphrates River into an irrigation canal simply by using existing flood control systems. This allowed the major part of the attacking Persian army to march into Babylon through a dried-up river bed, which went right under the city wall and through the middle of the city. Unopposed, they conquered Babylon within a matter of hours.

While reading further in the New Testament, I was very disturbed when I learned that the Euphrates River is to be diverted again (Revelation 16:12)! This is supposed to occur when the "Kings of the East," commanding two hundred million soldiers, invade Israel in the last and greatest battle of history. I had heard first of this battle when I was a little boy. It is called Armageddon.

Then another thought overcame me: *What is going to happen to the many predictions that these prophets of God have forecast for the future? Are they yet to occur? When?* I knew I should study these also. If they always had been true in the past, then I had better pay attention to them for the future.

Today, one reason why religious Jews can be seen praying so vehemently at the Wailing Wall is because they have been waiting for their Messiah for over two thousand years (Hosea 3:4). The prophecies concerning persecution of the Jews for disobedience and apostasy have been taking place for two thousand years, starting when God first permitted millions of Jews to be destroyed by the Roman general Titus in A.D. 70. Then the Jews were driven into a worldwide dispersion, now called Diaspora (Deuteronomy 28:63–68). Following this Jewish dispersion for worshiping other gods, God visited the Gentiles to take out of them a people for His name (Acts 15:14).

FUTURE PROPHECY

Having stated that He was a "jealous God," God told His chosen people that He would "persecute them through other nations" (Ezekiel 14:6–11 and Exodus 32:21–28), until the "times of the Gentiles [the control of Jerusalem by Gentile nations] are fulfilled" (Luke 21:24). This would occur in the "latter days." Finally, this "time of the Gentiles" was fulfilled when Israel became a nation again in 1948 and then occupied and claimed control of Jerusalem in May 1967. This fulfillment was actually predicted twenty-five hundred years before it occurred! It was so important that God recorded it at different times through four different prophets.

1. Deuteronomy 30:3: " 'then the LORD your God

will . . . gather you again from all the nations where he scattered you.' "

2. Isaiah 11:12: "He will raise a banner for the nations and gather the exiles of Israel; he will assemble the scattered people of Judah from the four quarters of the earth."

3. Amos 9:15: " 'I will plant Israel in their own land, never again to be uprooted from the land I have given them,' says the LORD your God."

4. Ezekiel 39:28: " 'Then they [the Jews] will know that I am the LORD their God, for though I sent them into exile among the nations, I will gather them to their own land, not leaving any behind. I will no longer hide my face from them, for I will pour out my Spirit on the house of Israel, declares the Sovereign LORD.' "

Since the nation of Israel was not again in existence until 1948 and there was no other such country by that name, still another bewildering prophecy could not have been completed until after Israel was established as a nation. Now it can occur. This concerns the prophesied invasion of Israel, apparently by Russia. (See Ezekiel 38 and 39.) This could never have taken place before our lifetime! The prophecy could only be fulfilled after 1948. It is possible that some of us will be alive to see it. The prophets assure us that it will occur.

Further explanation of biblical prophecy I will leave to the experts. Among the voluminous amount of literature available on this fascinating subject, I have found four sources that I highly recommend: several books by Hal Lindsey; many summaries by the evangelist, Jack Van Impe (*Israel's Final Holocaust* is one); *The Bible and To-*

morrow's News by Charles Ryrie; and "The Bible in the News," by Southwest Radio Church of Oklahoma City by David Webber, Noah Hutchings, and Emil Gaverluk. (Webber and Hutchings authored a book on this topic entitled *Is This the Last Century?*)

THINGS TO COME

Before death comes, careful preparation should naturally be made. Meanwhile, in light of current events, other important and urgent preparations should be made. Let me mention a few trends that seem consistent with the Bible's description of "end times."

Not in all of the centuries of history has the explosion of knowledge paralleled that of recent times. Within our lifetime, science has penetrated more barriers than in all preceding centuries. Technology has advanced further in this age than in all of man's existence.

This spectacular increase in knowledge suggests we may be approaching the Bible's predicted end times when "knowledge shall be increased," as emphasized in Daniel's well-known prophecy: "But you, Daniel, close up and seal the words of the scroll, until the time of the end. Many will go here and there to increase knowledge."[1]

In 1939 came the splitting of the atom and the release of nuclear energy, followed by probing discoveries in both the microcosm and macrocosm; nuclear submarines for year-round operation; computer systems for storing vast amounts of data; satellites to investigate outer space; rockets for reaching other planets; spaceships for orbiting the earth; radio telescopes to map the

[1]Daniel 12:4.

heavens; radioisotopes to kill cancers; antibiotics to cure bacterial diseases; and synthetic plastic substitutes for parts of the human body (plastic joints, plastic blood vessels, plastic heart valves, plastic eye lenses). The new discoveries made in our lifetime are so numerous that it is increasingly difficult for a scientist to keep up with new data even limited to his own field.

Since so much knowledge has been unearthed in the latter half of the present century, scientists more often than theologians have begun to predict an impending doom in our age. They warn us of our destructive pollution, our contamination of both the atmosphere and the earth by radioactive materials, our population explosion, and our propagation of various forms of nuclear destruction. Besides what we're doing to ourselves, each of us is becoming aware that nature is on a progressive rampage with droughts and famines, earthquakes and floods, hurricanes and pestilences.

Our newspapers today are confirming exactly what Christ predicted would happen when the end is near. In the Bible it is stated there would be ". . . famines, pestilences, and earthquakes in various places. All these are the beginning of sorrows."[2]

The momentum toward other tragic changes is also becoming more ominous. The fact that we are running out of energy and food, polluting the water, the earth, and the heavens, and even destroying the ozone layer that protects us against the killer rays of the sun—these have all caused us to wonder how long we have left.

In 1975 there were about four billion people on earth, and the average age of the world's citizens was thirty.

[2]Matthew 24:7,8.

The more developed and relatively affluent areas—North America, Japan, Russia, Europe, and New Zealand—had only twenty-seven percent of the population. At the same time the have-not nations represented seventy-three percent of the population!

FALSE PROPHETS

As they quote psychic prognostications of national events and other happenings, some people who follow the psychics seem to revere them as prophets of God. But the power of these prophets, although frequently virile and potent, is not from God.

Some psychics now are experimenting with unseen spirits. Often aided by drugs, they are opening Pandora's box to release satanic powers that may actually assist them in their predictions of the future.

Let's look at some letters from "Maria's Mail Bag," which appears in a widely read national newspaper.

Question: "I love your predictions and your accent. I am a Frenchborn Taurus in love with a Virgo. We love each other, but he is always sick. Can you tell me why this is so?"

Answer: "My own accent comes from being born in Portugal and being educated in Spain and France. I'm really like minestrone soup with various ingredients and spices. Your boyfriend loves you, and he will marry you. Take him to his family doctor as soon as possible. Tell the doctor that his infection is a kidney infection due to bacteria in his blood. The doctor will know what I'm talking about. Psychic healing cannot help him—he needs a doctor."

Question: "I am a Cancer and my mother says I have

had a Voodoo spell put on me by a band of gypsies so that I will lose all my boyfriends. Do you believe in Gypsy curses and Voodoo? Am I really sick and doomed to lose my boyfriends for the rest of my life?"

Answer: "You are definitely not sick. It is just that your mother is trying to punish you and you believe her. As a psychic, I know the gypsies, and those who practice Voodoo would not do this to you. Voodoo is a type of religion found in Haiti in the Caribbean and not a spell or a love breaker. Just stop giving yourself away and your next boyfriend will marry you."[3]

Everyone has problems. As a result psychics are in a very lucrative business. Some of these clairvoyants are using astrology, tarot cards, Ouija boards, palm readings, phrenology, and other mystic arts of the occult for information sources. These so-called prophets do not represent God. God specifically calls them "detestable" (Deuteronomy 18:10–12).

Peter, shortly before his martyrdom, warned that many teachers would be in the field of teaching and forecasting, including immoral and depraved false prophets parading in religious garb (*vis-a-vis*, Jim Jones, Father Divine, Reverend Sun Moon, etc.). Many would actually scoff at the thought of Jesus' coming again (2 Peter 3:3,4).

In similar fashion before his own martyrdom, Paul warned Timothy, "Preach the word! Be ready in season, out of season. . . . For the time will come when they will not endure sound doctrine, but according to their own desires, because they have itching ears, they will heap up for themselves teachers."[4] The Epistle of Jude in its

[3]"Maria's Mail Bag," *National Examiner* (December 26, 1978), p. 15.
[4]2 Timothy 4:2,3.

entirety is also dedicated to warning us against false teachers who are already in our midst.

Some of these false teachers have already become apparent to many. For instance, the Reverend Jim Jones made sure that he had everything going for him besides his charismatic charm. Using false promises to lure people into his assembly, he is said to have staged miracles to convince his followers that he was divinely appointed. One of his closest followers said that he used a mixture of chicken liver and blood, which after a "healing" he would hold up to the audience as a postoperative specimen and say, "Don't get close—that's cancer!" Then he would present the supposedly healed victim to the audience.

Claiming to be the reincarnation of Jesus, Jim Jones also had the habit of preaching with small plastic bags of blood hidden in his hands that he would "pop" to show where Christ-like wounds occurred in his hands. It is said he would hide his aides in special crawl spaces in the ceiling where they would pretend to be "spirit voices" who would answer when Jones allegedly conversed with beings from the "other side."

As other examples, most of us recall Charles Manson and people like Reverend Sun Moon and even Hitler himself—all who have been accused of using brainwashing techniques to induce people to submit to organizational orders and fanatical practices.

Changes in theology, doctrinal distortions by ministers of the faith, and abandonment of the Word of God by many who claim to be Christian leaders have appeared in most traditional faiths. At the same time atheism has been advanced as an alternative to biblical truth by using those same ancient practices of the Chaldeans and Babylonians that God strictly forbade—astrology and fortune-telling (Deuteronomy 1810–14).

We're seeing one of the significant predictions in the Bible coming true today. The apostle Paul was another of God's prophets. He said, ". . . *The Spirit expressly says in latter times some will depart from the faith, giving heed to deceiving spirits and doctrines of demons*" (italics added).[5] Right now we find respectable people following spirit beings and using spirit guides. Some of them are calling upon mystic messengers, totally unaware that these bland-appearing practices are employing the occult forces of evil.

THE POINT OF IT ALL

The thing we need to remember, then, is this: The prophetic Scriptures speaking to events that have *already* happened in history have been impeccably on target. There has been no margin of error. Therefore, it is safe to assume that biblical predictions dealing with events yet to come will be fulfilled in like manner.

Do you want to know your future? Don't consult mediums and psychics; consult the Bible. God's prophets have always been accurate.

How should you prepare to die? The first essential step is to know what to believe, since *your decision* involves *your life.*

Without question, prophecy establishes the truth of the Bible itself. If we know the Bible is true, then we are sure that death's door does open to heaven or hell—and Jesus Christ is the One who has the keys.

[5]2 Timothy 4:1.

CHAPTER XI
How to Conquer Death

In the first part of this book we dealt with the problems of death and dying. In the second part we have been concerned with a personal search for the answers to life after death—what to believe and why.

Examining the holy books of many world religions and offshoot cults, we found that prophecy is the insignia of God that establishes the veracity of only one book, the Bible. We looked at scientific experiments and various opinions and found that there is a growing belief in creation and the existence of God. Eternity is the long-questioned entity of the Bible that defines the spirit world and the abode of heaven and hell. My patients say eternity is there. Scriptures say it's there.

Just as God exists, eternity exists, and heaven and hell exist, so also does judgment exist. In fact the patients who have returned from the other side of death's door find themselves more concerned with judgment than with death.

Together with false prophets who ". . . secretly bring in destructive heresies,"[1] a resurgence of pagan religious beliefs has become apparent in our culture. These

[1] 2 Peter 2:1.

religions mold God into man's image and incorporate the pleasant benefits of all other religions. Reincarnation is the "answer" to life after death: Everybody gets in and no salvation is required "because there is no hell." Thus the birth of the new world religion has now appeared, which was predicted for end times.

What it boils down to is this question: Is man basically good and will he be reincarnated in a life on earth, or is man lost and in need of a redeemer before he is judged in eternity?

The Christian faith gives only one choice for man's salvation: "Nor is there salvation in any other, for there is no other name under heaven given among men by which we must be saved."[2] What name? Jesus Christ! Jesus Christ has the keys through death's door, for He said, " . . . 'I am the way, the truth, and the life. No one comes to the Father except through Me.' "[3]

Himself a physician, St. Luke, told us about the God to worship and to hold in fearful reverence:

> "And I say to you, My friends, do not be afraid of those who kill the body, and after that have no more that they can do. But I will warn you whom you should fear: Fear Him who, after He has killed, has power to cast into hell; yes, I say to you, fear Him!"[4]

WHO'S REALLY RIGHT ABOUT DEATH?

Have you ever noticed that when people are angry, they use the Christian God's name in vain? It's "God" this, and "Christ" that. I have met scores of international

[2]Acts 4:12.
[3]John 14:6.
[4]Luke 12:4,5.

students and physicians. Never once have I heard one say, "Buddha dammit" or "For Confucius' sake."

Nor have I *ever* heard anyone cry out to *anyone* but Jesus Christ on his deathbed. Not Krishna, not Mohammed, not Mary Baker Eddy, not one of the other religious leaders. Why not? Could this have anything to do with the fact that you can take a pilgrimage to the grave of the founders of all of the other religions of the world and pay homage to them in their resting place? They are known as being *dead*. But in the case of Jesus Christ, we are dealing with One who is *alive*. His grave is *empty*. He has conquered death and is seated at the right hand of the Father as Lord and King!

Many of my dying patients confront me with these very issues—questions vital to our destiny, which must be settled by each of us when facing death.

Some people have asked me, "But how do you know Jesus Christ told us the truth?" My answer is, "Because He is who He said He is—the eternal Son of God."

THE CREDENTIALS OF CHRIST

Anyone can make claims. Talk is cheap. However, Jesus had the credentials to back up His claims. He said, " '. . . though you do not believe Me, believe the works that you may know and believe that the Father is in Me, and I in Him.' "[5]

Of all the religious leaders, Christ alone claimed deity. The founders of all other religions emphasize their *teachings*. Not so with Christ. He made *Himself* the focal point of His teaching.

What were His credentials?

[5]John 10:38.

1. *His character on earth was holy because He is fully God.* Christ was *sinless*. He was able to challenge His enemies with the question, " 'Which of you convicts Me of sin? . . .' "[6] They gave no answer. We can note also, when we read the temptations of Christ, that we never hear of a confession of sin on His part. He never asked for forgiveness, although He told His followers to do so.

The righteousness of Jesus Christ is summarized well by Paul Little in his book *Know Why You Believe.*

> This lack of any sense of moral failure on Jesus' part is astonishing in view of the fact that it is completely contrary to the experience of the saints and mystics of all ages. The closer men and women draw to God the more overwhelmed they are with their own failure, corruption and shortcomings. The closer one is to a shining light, the more he realizes his need of a bath.[7]

It is also significant that the apostles John, Paul, and Peter speak of the sinlessness of Christ " 'Who committed no sin, Nor was guile found in His mouth,' "[8] "in . . . Him there is no sin,"[9] and Jesus "knew no sin."[10] Even the skeptics recognized the sinlessness of the Son of God. Pilate, no friend of Jesus, said: "What evil has He done?" And the Roman centurion, who was of necessity a judge of the character of men and who personally witnessed the death of Christ, said: ". . .'truly this was the Son of God!' "[11]

[6]John 8:46.
[7]Paul E. Little, *Know Why You Believe* (Wheaton, Ill.: Scripture Press, 1967), pp. 54–55.
[8]1 Peter 2:22.
[9]1 John 3:5.
[10]2 Corinthians 5:21.
[11]Matthew 27:54.

2. *Jesus Christ had controlling power over natural forces of the earth.* This power could only belong to God, the author of these forces. He stilled the raging storm on the Sea of Galilee so that those in the boat asked, ". . .'What kind of Man is this, that even the wind and the sea obey Him!' "[12] He also turned the water into wine, fed five thousand people from five loaves of bread and two fish, gave a grieving widow back her only son by raising him from the dead, and brought back to life the daughter of a shattered father. To an old friend He said, "Lazarus come forth!" Dramatically, the man came out of the tomb.

It is most significant that *His enemies did not deny these miracles.* Instead, because His actions made Him suspect of being divine, they tried to kill Him. " 'If we let Him alone like this, everyone will believe in Him. . . .' "[13] Demonstrating His divine power over sickness and disease, Jesus the great Physician made the lame to walk, the dumb to speak, and the blind to see. On some occasions He healed irreversible congenital problems and gross deformities that would have not been subject to imaginary or "psychosomatic" cures.

3. *The supreme credential authenticating Jesus' claim to deity was His resurrection from the dead.* In the course of His life He predicted five times that He would die. He even predicted *how* He would die and when He would rise from the dead to appear to His disciples.

The New Testament contains six independent accounts that verify the fact of the Resurrection. Three of those who saw Jesus alive after His death were John,

---

[12]Mark 4:41.
[13]John 11:48.

Peter, and Matthew. Paul, writing later to the churches, refers to the Resurrection in such a way that it is obvious that the event was well-known and accepted without question by the people.

GOD'S WITNESSES

Were these who witnessed the deity of Jesus Christ liars? Each of Christ's disciples faced the test of torture and martyrdom for his statements and beliefs. Throughout history men have died for what they *believed* to be true, though it actually may have been false. But men will not die for something that they *know* to be a lie!

Furthermore, several distinct appearances of Christ are recorded from the morning of His resurrection to His ascension forty days later. These accounts show a great variety as to time, place, and the people involved. Two appearances were to individuals, Peter and James. There were appearances to eleven of the disciples as a group; and one appearance was to "five hundred brethren at once."[14] The appearances were at different places. Some were in the garden near His tomb, some were in the upper room. One was on the road from Jerusalem to Emmaus, and some were far away in Galilee. Each appearance was characterized by different acts and words of Jesus.

Deliberate lies or unfounded hallucinations would be excluded by this variety of exposure in time and place and by the large number of people who saw Jesus after His resurrection. Hallucinations, for instance, usually occur only at one particular time and place and are associated with the events fancied. By contrast, the ap-

[14]1 Corinthians 15:6.

pearances of Christ were unpredicted and occurred both indoors and outdoors and in the morning, afternoon, and evening. Nevertheless, even the disciples upon seeing Him thought they were having hallucinations. This explains why Jesus finally had to tell them ". . . handle Me and see, for a spirit does not have flesh and bones as you see I have."[15] He also asked them if they had any food, and they gave Him a piece of broiled fish. In a resurrected body, he was still capable of eating!

I thank God for Thomas who is often called "the doubter" by us moderns. I identify with him. He said in effect, "I won't believe unless I am shown. I'm from Missouri. Show me!" In John 20:25, Thomas said, ". . . 'Unless I see in His hands the print of the nails, put my finger into the print of the nails, and put my hand into his side, I will not believe.' " Thomas was skeptical.

Eight days later Jesus appeared before Thomas and said,

> . . . "Reach your finger here, and look at My hands; and reach your hand here, and put it into My side. And do not be unbelieving, but believing." And Thomas answered and said to Him, "My Lord and my God."[16]

Was it just a *myth*, then, that changed this band of frightened, cowardly disciples into men of courage and conviction? Was it personal whim or naked fact that changed Peter from one who, the night before the Crucifixion, was so afraid for his own life that he denied three times that he even knew Jesus? Was it daydream or reality that confronted Peter, changing him into the pil-

[15]Luke 24:39.
[16]John 20:27,28.

lar of faith who, some fifty days later, risked his life by saying that he had seen the resurrected Jesus?

The good news for you and me is that if Jesus Christ rose from the dead, then He is alive today—powerful enough to invade and change our lives. Of all of God's miracles, the greatest was the Resurrection.

Oh, I know that proving a miracle in the laboratory requires reproducibility. But even if this were physically possible, the doubters would still make a rationalistic presupposition to rule out a miracle even if they saw one! They would appeal to their "reason" and say, "No! Miracles are impossible!" No amount of evidence would ever persuade them one had taken place. It would be as Jesus recounted in Luke 16 when the rich man protested that someone should rise from the dead and tell his five brothers that hell is a real place—so that they wouldn't arrive at the same place where the rich man was and would believe that there is a life after death. But Father Abraham said, " '. . ."If they do not hear Moses and the prophets, neither will they be persuaded though one rise from the dead." ' "[17] In other words, they wouldn't believe even if someone came back to life to tell them about life after death. And this is what I believe is happening today!

We who insist on seeing everything firsthand realize that almost every judicial court in the world operates on the basis of *testimony*, either by word of mouth or by written document. The decision to take a person's life may be based on testimony.

As described by Paul Little, the raising of Martha's brother, Lazarus, from the dead was one of many great

[17]Luke 16:31.

miracles Jesus did in public. This event was seen by many and actually witnessed and faithfully recorded by the apostle John. Furthermore, it is impressive that the opponents of Jesus never denied that He had performed miracles. Instead, they attributed them to Satan, or otherwise tried to suppress the evidence, as they did when Lazarus was raised from the dead. They finally decided that He must be killed before the people realized what was happening and the whole world followed Him. (See John 12:19.)

The crux of the matter is this: Did these eyewitness observers who saw Jesus Christ after His resurrection tell the truth? The answer is illustrated by the fact that most of these disciples, facing death as the test of their veracity, held tenaciously to the evidence. They bet their lives on it!

Yet people today reject God! Why? The apostle John told us that man prefers the darkness rather than the light because he does not want to change his life-style. He prefers what he considers the "good times." (See John 3:19.)

Transient pleasures of sex and drugs pervade man's search for ultimate satisfaction. Lasting peace, however, evades our grasp as we attempt to quench the desires of our immortal soul at the human fountain of materialism. The adulterer and the alcoholic, the abuser and the addict, all are looking for ultimate satisfaction that can be supplied only by Christ who dispenses abundant security. He said, ". . .'I am the light of the world. He who follows Me shall not walk in darkness, but have the light of life.' "[18]

[18]John 8:12.

The limited satisfactions of drugs, sex, and money do not fulfill our lasting desires. The late psychologist Carl Gustav Jung once said that "the central neurosis of our time is emptiness." We think that money, fame, success, power, or other externals will achieve our ultimate internal happiness. But after we attain them we learn too late that the experiences are disillusioning. The realization occurs that we are still the same old, miserable person!

The human spirit can never be satisfied "by bread alone." Christ said, ". . .'I am the bread of life. He who comes to me shall never hunger, and he who believes in Me shall never thirst.' "[19] With Christ we can transcend circumstances.

And the Christian conversion solves our guilt problems. Guilt is a normal phenomenon and should not be rationalized away. Christianity addresses this convicting guilt of man. In spite of the population explosion, man remains more lonely than ever, seeking superficial pleasures to fill the gap. Guilt and loneliness create the depression that so often persists and erodes mental health. It is the "Jesus factor," the Christian experience, which has been found to be such a sound basis for mental health, a proven asset to the individual, and one of the rare cures for the emotionally destitute.

COMING TO FAITH

In all of this, a central message emerges: We must come to a place of faith, the surrender of our lives to the reign of Jesus Christ. This involves turning from our own thing, from running our lives ourselves, to commit-

[19]John 6:35.

ting ourselves to Jesus as Lord. Doing so makes us ready both for life now and for death later on.

Among my recent patients was a little girl who was dying. Her mother was praying daily for her recovery; however, the little girl's condition was becoming worse. Finally one evening, during her mother's prayer for the child's recovery, the little girl interrupted her mother. "Quit praying for me. I am tired and I am ready to die. I am not afraid of dying," she said.

The relief of the mother was overwhelming. She stopped quoting Scriptures in her prayers to support what *she* wanted and asked that God's will be done. Instead of trying to manipulate God, she still told Him what she wanted—but she did so stating her submission to His will.

In the few remaining days of the child's life, the two of them talked about the daughter's nearing departure and her future, based on her relationship to Jesus Christ. This allowed the child to die in an atmosphere of love and understanding, which replaced the hysteria and the panic that previously had pervaded the household. If the earlier course of events had continued, the girl would have been unprepared for death. Her predicament would have been similar to what most of us will face. We should not miss that once-in-a-lifetime chance to take time to comfort a loved one when death approaches instead of being too busy praying for him or her to have "another day of life."

What a difference Jesus Christ makes in our lives!

Now ask yourself a personal question. Are you a new creature in Christ? Have you really been "born again"? Or are you like I used to be, *the same old person?*

Do you know where you will spend eternity? What's

more important to you than your own life? What moment is more important to you than right now? The moment you were born? The moment you will die? *Right now may be the greatest moment in your whole life!* You can't buy this gift of eternal life—it's not even for sale! Although the gospel is "good news" now, for many it will be "bad news" later, when it will be too late!

You say you don't want to be bothered? You've been a Christian all your life? Well I used to say these things too. But have you also been, like me, a Christian of "convenience"? An "intellectual" Christian? A "lukewarm" Christian? Has your faith, like mine, been cold and dull and dead?

Although Christ was talking to the ancient churches, I am convinced He was also speaking to you and me when He said:

> " 'I know your works, that you are neither cold nor hot; I wish you were cold or hot. So then, because you are lukewarm, and neither cold nor hot, I will spew you out of My mouth. Because you say: I am rich, have become wealthy, and have need of nothing—and do not know that you are wretched, miserable, poor, blind, and naked.' "[20]

That described me! Does it describe you?

Yes, I will admit that I am rich. I confess it! I have my own airplane and my own lake house, but it really doesn't mean much. God says that without Him in actuality I am "poor and blind and naked."

But, thank God, He provided the answer just a few verses later in Revelation. He said: " 'Behold, I stand at

[20]Revelation 3:15–17.

the door and knock. *If anyone hears My voice and opens the door, I will come in to him and dine with him, and he with Me'* " (italics added).[21] God has given you and me the answer!

Do you want to "open" the door? He promised He would come in. If you want to commit your life to Jesus Christ for the first time or recommit your life to Him, you may say this prayer with me:

> Lord Jesus, I need You. Forgive me of my sins. I ask You to take over my life and make me the kind of person You want me to be. Thank You for forgiving my sins and for Your promise never to leave me. Fill me now with the Holy Spirit, so that I can do Your will and talk to You anytime, anywhere. Thank You for the gift of eternal life. And thank You especially for letting me know how important I am to You. Amen.

If you prayed this prayer sincerely—or you are already a believer in Christ—you can now be confident about your destination before death comes.

Do you remember what was said at the beginning of this book? "All through history man has been the only creature made aware that he must die. Yet he refuses to believe it until the last moment, when he is usually unprepared."

I'll close with this thought: *Likewise, man is the only creature made aware of salvation, and yet he refuses to accept it until the last moment, when it is sometimes too late.*

May God give you the softness of heart to turn to Him now.

[21]Revelation 3:20.

APPENDIX

Hospices in the United States

ARKANSAS

Hospice of Jonesboro
Jennifer Ayers, R.N., Treas.
Route 2, Box 182
Jonesboro, AR 72401

Northwest Arkansas
  Hospice Assn.
P.O. Box 817
Fayetteville, AR 72701
Elizabeth Sizer, Admin.

Hospice of the Ozarks
808 Church St.
Mountain Home, AR 72653
M. Carolyn Wilson, MD.

COLORADO

Boulder County Hospice, Inc.
2118 14th St.
Boulder, CO 80302
(303) 449-7740
Beau Bohart, Ph.D.

Grand River Hospital District
Harald Friesser, Admin.
701 East Fifth Street
Rifle, CO 81650

Hospice of Metro Denver
1719 E. 19th Ave., Rm. 256
Denver, CO 80218
(303) 839-6256
Betty L. Gordon, R.N.

Hospice Inc. of Larimer County
P.O. Box 957
Fort Collins, CO 80522
(303) 484-5494

CONNECTICUT

Hospice, Incorporated
765 Prospect St.
New Haven, CT 06511
(203) 787-5871
Dennis Rezendes

FLORIDA

The Elisabeth Kubler-Ross
  Hospice, Inc.
P.O. Box 6311
Clearwater, FL 33516
(813) 461-5125
Leo Gamon

Hospice of Boca Raton
% Unitarian Fellowship
162 W. Palmetto Park Rd.
Boca Raton, FL 33432

Hospice of Pensacola
8355 No. Davis Hwy.
Pensacola, FL 32504

Hospice of Miami
127 N.E. 4 Street
Miami, FL 33132
(305) 371-0927
Hugh Westbrook

Gold Coast Home Health
  Services, Inc.
4699 N. Federal Highway
Pompano Beach, FL 33064
Mary Fay Verville, RN

University Community Hospital
3100 E. Fletcher Ave.
Tampa, FL 33612

Hospice Orlando, Inc.
P.O. Box 8581
Orlando, FL 32806
(305) 647-2523
Dr. Daniel C. Hadlock

Hospice of Broward, Inc.
3700 Washington St. #208
Hollywood, FL 33021
Jane Herron, Admin.

Hospice of Palm Beach
  County, Inc.
P.O. Box 6562
W. Palm Beach, FL 33405
(305) 582-0143
Stella Monchick, R.N., B.H.S.

Halifax Hospital Medical Center
P.O. Box 1990
Daytona Beach, FL 32015
Dr. H. D. Kermen

Hospice of St. Francis, Inc.
P.O. Box 5563
Titusville, FL 32780
(305) 267-2842
Emilie Sasko, R.N.

Hospice of South Brevard, Inc.
P.O. Box 463
Melbourne, FL 32901
Martha Kaufman

Hospice of So. Florida
50 E. Las Olas Blvd.
Ft. Lauderdale, FL 33301
A. T. Parker, Jr.

GEORGIA

Hospice Atlanta, Inc.
P.O. Box 8376
Atlanta, GA 30306
(404) 881-6811
G. Harrison Hamily

Hospice of Savannah
P.O. Box 9119
Savannah, GA 31412

Wesley Homes, Inc.
1817 Clifton Rd., NE
Atlanta, GA 30329
(404) 325-2988
J. Scott Houston

Atlanta Hospital & Medical
  Center
705 Juniper Street NE
Atlanta, GA 30308
Mrs. Constance Lloyd, Admin.

HAWAII

Saint Francis Hospital
2230 Liliha Street

APPENDIX: HOSPICES IN THE UNITED STATES

Honolulu, HI 96817
(808) 547-6011
Sr. Maureen Keleher, F.A.C.H.A.

ILLINOIS

Evangelical Hospital
  Association (UCC)
1415 W. 22nd St.
Oak Brook, IL 60521
(312) 986-6399
Larry K. Ulrich

Hospice of Madison County
2120 Madison Ave.
Granite City, IL 62040
Shabbir Safdar, MD

Horizon Hospice, Inc.
2430 N. Lakeview
Chicago, IL 60614
(312) 327-8086
Ada Addington

Hospice of Highland
  Park Hospital
718 Glenview Ave.
Highland Park, IL 60015
(312) 432-8000
Mrs. T. Margaret Di Francesca,
  RN, Hospice Coordinator

INDIANA

Hospice of Southern Indiana
Joan Sauer, Program Developer
134 East Main Street
New Albany, IN 47150

Methodist Hospital of
  Indiana, Inc.
Hospice Care Unit
P.O. Box 1367

1604 N. Capitol Ave.
Indianapolis, IN 46206

Parkview Memorial Hospital
  Hospice
2200 Randalia Dr.
Fort Wayne, IN 46805
(219) 484-6636
Donald K. Reeves

KANSAS

Hadley Regional Medical Center
201 East Seventh Street
Hays, KS 67601
Chaplain Robert Pattie

Hospice, Inc. Topeka, Kansas
2530 NW Brickyard Rd.
Topeka, KS 66618
Eliz. Wooster

KENTUCKY

E. McDowell Community
  Hospice Program
915 South Limestone
Lexington, KY 40503
(606) 233-6541
Dr. Ann Blues

Hospice of Louisville
233 E. Grey St., Suite 604
Louisville, KY 40222
(502) 584-4834
Maryanne Werronen

LOUISIANA

Mercy Hospital
P.O. Box 19024
New Orleans, LA 70179
Sr. Mary Vernon, Dir. Soc. Svcs.

177

MICHIGAN

Battle Creek Sanitarium
Hospital
197 N. Washington Avenue
Battle Creek, MI 49016
Chaplain Larry Yeagley

Battle Creek Hospice Planning
Visiting Nurse Service of
Calhoun County
181 No. Ave.
Battle Creek, MI 49017
H. Armstrong

Hospice of Flint
806 W. Sixth Avenue
Flint, MI 48503

Visiting Nurse Service of Calhoun County
181 No. Ave.
Battle Creek, MI 49017
Margaret Armstrong, RN

MINNESOTA

Bethesda Lutheran Hospice
559 Capitol Blvd.
St. Paul, MN 55103
(612) 221-2376
Carmian M. Seifert, RN, MPH

North Memorial Medical Center
3220 Lowry Ave. N.
Minneapolis, MN 55422
Judith Kaplan, RN

Fairview-Southdale Hospital
6401 France Avenue, South
Minneapolis, MN 55435
D.N. Robinson

Riveredge Hospice
415 Oak St.

P.O. Box 313
Breckenridge, MN 56520
Sr. Mary Camillus Weier

St. Luke's Hospital
915 E. First St.
Duluth, MN 55805

NEW HAMPSHIRE

Seacoast Hospice
P.O. Box 237
Exeter, NH 03833

NEW YORK

St. Mary's Hospital for Children
2901 216th Street
Bayside, NY 11360
Jane Hoskovec, Admin.

Metropolitan Jewish Geriatric
Ctr.
4915 Tenth Ave.
Brooklyn, NY 11219
Eli Feldman

Hospice Buffalo, Inc.
2929 Main St.
Buffalo, NY 14214
(716) 838-4438
Charlotte N. Sheed, RN, MN

Hospice Care of Utica, NY
1 Pearl Street
New Hartford, NY 13413

Calvary Hospital
1740 Eastchester Rd.
Bronx, NY 10461
Lorraine Tredge, Admin.

Columbia Univ. Foundation of
Thanatology

APPENDIX: HOSPICES IN THE UNITED STATES

West Chester County Div. of
Hospice Program
730 Park Avenue
New York, NY 10021

Hospice of Rockland, Inc.
Rockland County Health Center
Pomona, NY 10970
(914) 354-0200
Joe Brass

Beekman Downtown Hospital
170 William St.
New York, NY 10038
Eloise Menzillo

Hospice of Westchester
% Community Unitarian
   Church
Roasedale Ave. & Sycamore
   Lane
White Plains, NY 01605

Mercy Hospital
1000 N. Village Ave.
Rockville Centre, NY 11570
Sr. Dolores Castelli

The Brooklyn Hospice
Metropolitan Jewish Geriatric
   Center
4915 Tenth Ave.
Brooklyn, NY 11219
(212) 853-2800
Dennis Kodner, Dir. of Planning

St. Luke's Hospital Center
Amsterdam Ave. at 114th St.
New York, NY 10025
(212) 870-1732 or 870-6000
Chaplain Carleton Sweetser

United Hospital Hospice
406 Boston Post Rd.
Port Chester, NY 10573

NORTH CAROLINA

Hospice at Charlotte, Inc.
Professional Services Center
403 N. Taylor St.
Charlotte, NC 28202
(704) 375-0100
Zach Thomas, III, Pres of the Bd.

Hospice of North Carolina, Inc.
P.O. Box 3112, Duke Univ. Med.
   Ctr.
Durham, NC 27710
(919) 724-7122
Peter Keese

SOUTH CAROLINA

Greenville Hospital System
701 Grove Road
Greenville, SC 29605
Mrs. Nancy Archer, Asst.
   Admin.

S.C. Baptist Hospital
Taylor at Marion Sts.
Columbia, SC 29220
Lynn O'Brien

TENNESSEE

Hospice of Memphis
First United Methodist Church
204 No. Second St.
Memphis, TN 38105

TEXAS

Home Health-Home Care, Inc.
904 N. 28th St.
Orange, TX 77630
(713) 886-0141
Louise Jones Maberry

179

St. Joseph Hospital
1401 South Main Street
Fort Worth, TX 76104
(817) 336-9371
Mary Mullins, Asst. Dir.

Trinity Valley Hospice Assoc.
4920 Reynolds Rd.
Fort Worth, TX 76118
Clyde Zeelers, Treas.

Ann's Haven
Hospice of Denton County
P.O. Box 856
Denton, TX 76201

Ecumenical Center of Religion &
    Health
4507 Medical Drive
San Antonio, TX 78229

The Southeast Texas Hospice
312 W. Pine
Orange, TX 77630
(713) 886-0622
Peggy McKenna

Girling & Assoc. Home Health
    Service
1404 N. Loop
Austin, TX 78755

St. Benedict's Hospice
330 E. Johnson
San Antonio, TX 78201

WASHINGTON

Hospice of Seattle
821 Boylston
Seattle, WA 98104
(206) 322-1881
Elaine McIntosh

Hospice of Tacoma
742 Market St. #201
Tacoma, WA 98402
(206) 383-4153
Anne M. Katterhagen, RN, BSN

WEST VIRGINIA

Foundation of Hospice of the
    Greater Upper Ohio Valley
30 Hamilton Ave.
Wheeling, WV 26003
Rev. Charles Elwood